Discovering the Hidden Gems of Kyoto: Insider's Guide

Emmie .E Macgregor

Funny helpful tips:

The world is a canvas of endless possibilities; paint your life with bold strokes and vibrant colors.

Stay adventurous; stepping out of comfort zones often leads to growth.

Discovering the Hidden Gems of Kyoto: Insider's Guide : Uncovering Kyoto's Best Kept Secrets: Essential Guide for Authentic Travels.

Life advices:

Stay vigilant about cybersecurity; protecting data is crucial in the digital age.

Network actively; connections can open doors to opportunities and collaborations.

Introduction

This book provides comprehensive information and insights for travelers planning to visit the enchanting city of Kyoto, Japan. The guide covers various aspects of Kyoto, including festivals, cultural events, the best time to travel, different regions to explore, must-visit attractions, day-by-day itineraries, transportation options, accommodation choices, local cuisine, and practical tips for a memorable trip.

The guide begins with an overview of the festivals and cultural events that take place in Kyoto, giving travelers a glimpse into the vibrant traditions and celebrations of the city. It also highlights the best time to travel to Kyoto, considering weather conditions and the timing of popular events.

Next, the guide provides a glance at different regions of Kyoto, such as the Nishijin District, Shinkyogoku District, Gion District, Northern Kyoto, Southern Kyoto, and Western Kyoto District. Each region is described briefly, giving travelers an idea of what to expect and which areas to explore based on their interests.

The "Must Dos" section presents a list of essential experiences in Kyoto. From climbing up the Kyoto Tower to having a photo op at Fushimi Inari Shrines, visiting temples and shrines, wandering in the Bamboo Forest, joining a tea ceremony, riding a traditional rickshaw, feeding snow monkeys, meditating at Ryoanji Temple, and more, this section offers a variety of captivating activities for travelers to enjoy.

For those seeking more structured itineraries, the "Day by Day Itineraries" section provides detailed plans for exploring Kyoto over a span of days, making it easier for travelers to maximize their time and visit the most iconic places.

The guide covers the basics of traveling in Kyoto, including transportation options and the best places to stay. It introduces different types of accommodation, such as ryokans, hotels, business hotels, and bed and breakfast options, while also providing ryokan etiquette to help travelers understand traditional Japanese inn customs.

Delving into Kyoto's culinary delights, the guide highlights Kyoto-style sushi, Shojin Ryori (Buddhist vegetarian cuisine), tofu dishes, vegetarian soy milk ramen, and Kyo-wagashi (traditional Kyoto sweets). Travelers will find recommendations for local delicacies to savor during their visit.

"Need to Know" provides practical information and tips to help travelers navigate Kyoto smoothly, including essential maps and insights into local life. This section serves as a valuable resource for making the most of a trip to this culturally rich city.

Overall, this book serves as a comprehensive companion for travelers, equipping them with valuable knowledge to experience the best of Kyoto's cultural heritage, traditions, and picturesque landscapes.

Contents

Introduction

Brief History

Even though archaeological proof places the first human life in Japan to around 10,000 BC, relatively little is known about human activity in the area before the 6th century AD. On the 8th century, when the influential Buddhist ministry got involved in the undertakings of the Imperial government, the Emperor decided to move the capital to a region far from the Buddhist influence. Emperor Kammu chose the Uda village, during the time in the district of Kadono in Yamashito Province, to honor this.

The new city, Heian-kyō, became the imperial of Japan's court in 794, starting the period of Heian of Japanese history. Eventually, the city was changed its name to Kyoto. Kyoto remained the capital of Japan until the transfer of the government to Edo in the year 1868 during the time of the Imperial Restoration. After Edo's name changed to Tokyo, Kyoto was also named as Saikyo for a short time.

An old spelling of the name of the city is Kioto; it was previously known to the West as Miako or Meaco. Another term normally used to call the city in the pre-modern period was Keishi, which means "capital" or "metropolis."

The city has suffered wide destruction in the Ōnin War of 1467 to 1477 and didn't really recover until the mid-16th century. Battles between samurai groups slopped into the streets and came to involve the religious factions and court nobility as well. The mansions of Nobles were turned into fortresses, deep trenches excavated all over the city for defense and as firebreaks, and many buildings burned. The city hasn't seen such extensive destruction since. Even though there was some consideration by the United States of targeting Kyoto using an atomic bomb at the latter part of WWII, in the end, it was decided to take out the city from the list of targets because of the "beauty of the city," and the city was spared conventional bombing too.

Because of this, Kyoto is the only big city in Japan that still has a profusion of prewar structures, like the traditional townhouses like machiya. But modernization is repeatedly breaking down the old-style Kyoto all for newer architecture, like the Kyoto Station compound.

Kyoto became a city selected by government ordinance on September 1, 1956. In the year 1997, Kyoto held the conference that ensued in the procedure on greenhouse gas emissions that bears the name of the city.

A common pronunciation of Kyoto in English has three syllables as /key-oh-toe/ but the Japanese pronunciation has only two syllables which are /ko - to/.

Festivals and Cultural Events

Aoi Festival Parade

Kyoto is an old city that used to be Japan's capital for more than one millennium. A lot of the festivals and cultural events being celebrated in the city are historic reenactments that celebrate the glory days of Kyoto as the capital. Kyoto has a lot of seasonal attractions like cherry blossoms that make the city's shrines, temples, parks, palaces, and gardens more alive.

Below are some of the most prominent events in Kyoto.

January

Hatsumode (1 to 3) Hatsumode refers to the year's first shrine visit, where people are visiting different shrines all over Kyoto to pray for a good year and get omamori talismans as protections. One of the most famous places to go visit is Yasaka Shrine, where locals normally go out in their kimono.

Kemari-hajime (4) Kemari Hajime is an old game that resembles hacky-sack, made from a sack made of deer skin that is played at Shimogamo Shrine. Men wear Heian-period costume and crease in a circle to compete as viewers watch.

Hatsu-Ebisu (8 to 9) Ebisu, the god of merchants is visited at Ebisu shrine by people who have traded to pray for a prosperous New Year, getting a good luck bamboo branch to be exhibited in the place of work.

February

Setsubun (3) In Kyoto, Setsubun is held at different shrines, but the biggest celebration is at Yoshida Shrine, where on the evening of 2nd of February, demons of different colors signifying different bad luck are shunned away. The following day, talismans from the year are thrown in a fire seven meters high as a kind of "holy fire" to scare the demons away. Game and food stalls are a line on the front of the shrine on both days.

Godai Rikison-Nin-no-e (23) At Daigo-Ji temple, a special weight-lifting ceremony or contest is hosted wherein participants compete to see who can lift a 90-kilogram mochi rice cake for the longest amount of time. A divinity that stops theft is venerated on this day.

Baika-sai (25) Geisha and maiko host an open-air tea ceremony underneath the plum blossoms at Kitano-tenmangu Shrine. There's a special offering ceremony of plum blossoms for Heian era scholar Sugawara Michizane on this day which is also the same date of his death. Sugawara loved plum blossoms.

March

Hina Matsuri (3) Hina-matsuri is what known as Girl's day. It is also known as a doll's festival where families with little girls show a group of decorative dolls that represent the Heian court on a red platform. In old Japanese tradition, hina dolls were placed in a boat to float downstream to sea to take worries and bad spirits together with them. Kyoto celebrates the Nagashi-bina by floating these dolls between the Kamo Rivers and Takano to pray for the children's safety.

Hozugawa Kudari Kawa Biraki (10) This day is the opening day of this riverboat ride on the Hozugawa River to Arashiyama from Kameoka which goes until the month of November. The opening day consists of some interesting and fun events along with the boat ride. The ride itself covers 16-kilometer in 2 hours.

Hana Toro (10 to 21) In the area of Higashiyama, from Shoren-in Temple to Kiyomizu Temple, you'll see lanterns that are lined in the streets lighting the cherry blossoms overhead. Every temple in this area opens their doors to guests at night. Different events and performances are also held on certain days at participating shrines and temples.

April

Ohana-mi (Cherry-blossoms peak season) Cherry-blossom viewing is an exceptional Japanese custom, and the flowers are admired while they are at their best in a type of huge outdoor picnic below the trees. In Kyoto, there are tons of scenic places to engage in Ohana-mi. In Maruyama-koen, big groups assemble on a blue plastic tarp to have some meal and drink, and these festivities normally go late into the night, the crowds get wilder as people get drunker.

May

Aoi Matsuri (15) Aoi Matsuri is one of the three main festivals in Kyoto hosted by Kamigamo and Shimogamo shrines. This is more of a procession than a festival, though, people in radiantly colored attires of the ancient Heian court march down the streets of the city, some on horseback, some walking alongside attractively ornamented carriages. The procession begins at the Imperial palace, making a stop at Shimogamo shrine in the south and ending at Kamigamo shrine.

Uesaku Matsuri (Night of the Full Moon) On May's full moon, Kuruma Temple hosts this festival in devotion to the Buddhist guardian god, Bishamonten. It's the only Himalayan-style full moon event in the country. The participants are praying and offerings of fresh water to the moon and a host of lanterns are ignited.

Mifune Matsuri Festival (Third Sunday) This event is held on Oigawa in Arashiyama and is hosted by neighboring Kurumazaki shrine, recognized for its deity of the performing arts. Three main boats bring people dressed in Heian court dress chanting poetry, playing instruments, and performing Noh plays or dancing. These boats lead 30 other smaller boats that also carry costumed performers.

June

Nagashi Oharai Festival (30) Nagoshi Harae is a religious practice that is believed to keep one safe from the hot summer and be safe from any disease and natural disasters. You can see Nagoshi Harae being practiced at local shrines in most parts of the city. The practice might vary depending on which shrine you go to but they have the same idea. Normally, a big wreath is made out of Japanese grasslands and it's said to cleanse you if you walk through it three times.

Kawadoko Kawadoko is being heled every summer from the month of June to August. Annually, carpenters will construct wooden balconies throughout the riverbanks of Kyoto for people to sit and relax while having a dinner on a hot summer evening. There are shrines that have different names for it. Nouryoudoko is essentially the same meaning as kawadoko.

July

Tanabata Festival (7) This children's festival rejoices the meeting of Hikoboshi and Orihime. The Milky Way, a river made of stars divides these lovers, and they're just allowed to meet one time a year. During this day, kids write their wishes, sometimes in poetry form known as tanzaku, on paper decorations and to decorate the bamboo branches.

Yoiyama Festival (14) Yoiyama festival is held on the eve of Gion Matsuri. It's one of biggest attractions of Kyoto. More than 400,000 people gather together that eve to watch the city embodied before one of biggest festivals of Japan takes place. Large city streets and roads get choked off for the mass pedestrian flow. It's even hard for bikers to pass through the crowd.

Gion Matsuri (15 to 17) Gion Matsuri is one of the grandest festivals celebrated in the whole country. It's celebrated to hold off bad omens like natural disasters and diseases. Dating back to the late 6th century, Gion matsuri was done as a religious cleansing ceremonial, but by the Kamakura period, it had become a way for craft merchants to show off their wealth.

The Mitarashi Matsuri (20 to 23) Mitarashi Matsuri rejoices the cleansing powers of a deity preserved at Shimogamo Shrine. During the evening, one wades into knee deep water in the stream that flows through the shrine, illuminating a candle at an end which leaves it on a special tiered pedestal at the other side.

Tanukidanisan Hiwatari ritual (28) During the evening, prayer sticks are lit and visitors are led by mountain priests to walk on burning coals. The fire-walk is safe for every participant and serves to cleanse the worshipper and offer defense from illness. Defensive paper talismans are given out in the end.

August

Manto and Sento Ceremonies (5 to 20) These memorial services held during Obon for the spirits of the dead. By the flaming lights of thousands of candles or lanterns, people ask their ancestors to guide them. Manto ceremonies could be seen at a lot of major temples throughout Kyoto, and every temple displays their numerous lanterns in different ways.

Toki Matsuri (7 to 10) A 3-day festival, Gojo dori east of Kamogawa comes alive in the boiling heat with the craftsman that sells Kiyomizu-yaki ceramics and pottery at slightly cut-rate prices. Stalls line either side of the street from noontime to evening, and normally one can talk directly with the maker of the wares you see.

Daimonji Gozan no Okuribi (16) Five huge symbols, four kanji characters, and a simple boat shape are set afire on the hills that surround Kyoto and can be seen from main places in Kyoto. The practice started from lighting fires at the end of Obon Festival of Souls to guide one's inherited spirits who have come down to earth back homeward to heaven.

Jizo bon (22 to 23) The Jizo-Bon festival is unique to Kyoto and takes place the weekend following the Obon holidays. These are the same as neighborhood block parties that serve as a type of children's festival to pray for the children's health. Expansive over two days, temporary altars are set up, and the neighborhood is decorated with food stalls, paper lanterns, and children participate in light fireworks, games, and eat sweets while adults converse for drink and conversation.

September

Otsuki-mi (5 to 7) Different events occur over three days in September in different temples and shrines around the city to admire the harvest moon. At Shimogamo shrine, Meigetu-kangen-sai is held, this is where people gather to watch the full moon while ancient court music is playing with Japanese instruments. At

Daikakuji temple, an event known as Kangetsu-no-yube is held, and flowers are devoted to the Bodhisattva of Moonlight in the main hall.

Kiyomizu dera Seiryu-ue (15 to 17) A dragon, is believed to drink the waterfall in Kiyomizu Temple. You will see a sparkling parade of the blue dragon with people wearing traditional attire at 2:00 in the afternoon.

October

Jidai Matsuri (22) The Jidai Matsuri, which is one of the largest festivals in the city, marks the date when the country's capital was moved to Kyoto in 794. It's known as the Festival of Ages, as it portrays the people in Japanese history straddling the Heian to Meiji era. Omikoshi of the first and last Kyoto Emperors lead about 2000 participants in beautiful ancient costume from different time periods travel in a 2-kilometer procession from The Imperial Palace to Heian Shrine.

Hatsuka Ebisu Festival (19 to 21) Businessmen go to Ebisu Shrine to buy fukuzasa, which a branch of bamboo ornamented with lucky charms. The branch is exhibited at one's business to help make sure an affluent future. Ebisu, one of the seven gods of good fortune and the patron deity of merchants is renowned.

Kurama Himatsuri (22) Himatsuri is a yearly fire festival that is held in Kurama, a little suburb in the northern of Kyoto. Originally, the festival made the way to light the path for the dead. Beginning at 6:00 PM, 3-meter tall watch fires known as kagaribi are ignited at once in the lead of homes.

November

Autumn Private Viewing (1 to 11) A lot of valuables that are normally not available for public viewing are exhibited on this day in the city supported by the Kyoto cultural preservation association center. Put on exhibition, will be such things as the construction of the garden parks, temple, and jewelry. To see these main artifacts is a really popular event and people hope for it each year. Throughout this period, you can come and see the artifacts without the need of any reservation, unless you're visiting with a big group, then you need to make an early reservation.

Annual Gion Dance (Beginning of November) This is an exhibition of Old workmanship and presentations of stylish country Gion Folk songs will be presented. You are able to get experience autumn entertainment of this former country's capital.

December

Joya no Kane (31) This is the New Year's Eve and before midnight, a lot of temples ring their bells 108 times. In Buddhism, it's believed that human beings have 108 earthy desires that cause sufferings for humans. Listening to every ring of the bell can help in rid their sins, beginning of the New Year with a fresh heart and mind.

Okeramairi (31) At Yasaka Shrine, midnight on New Year's Eve, the roots of the Okera, a medicinal plant, are set ablaze, and lanterns in many locations in the shrine are lit using this fire. Okera is said to cast off the evil energy of the past year and offer a long life. It's a custom for visitors to take home the ashes of the fire by always swinging a bamboo rope lit with the fire, which is then used to cook a mochi soup, ozoni, or to light a candle for the alter at home.

Shimai Tenjin/Shimai Kobo (21 and 25) On the 21st and 25th of this month, a big flea market is set up at To-ji and Kitano-tenmangu Shrine Temple respectively. A lot of stalls fill the grounds that sell antiques, food, kimonos, and other stuff. The year-end markets are larger than those held the rest of the year, and stock up quickly so go as early as you can in order to avoid the big crowds.

Best Time to Travel

As a traveler, there are many factors that go with planning for your trip. Of course, you can simply fly, get to your hotel, and just see where your feet take you. But when you do this, you could miss out on many things in Kyoto, Japan if you do not perform a bit due diligence beforehand.

It is not surprising that the most popular times to travel to Kyoto is when the climate is the most stable and pleasing. The months of **March up to May** are best months to visit as these months are when things are starting to get warm and are most comfortable for any tourists. The months of **October and November** throughout the **autumn season** are similarly desirable as it is sunny and warm during the day and the evenings are pleasingly cool.

When visiting in **April**, you will also have the chance to witness the Cherry Blossom Festival, but remember that the city gets crowded with locals and foreign tourists during this time. In the same way, the charming autumn foliage creates high numbers of tourists. Because of this, it's important for you to make a hotel reservation beforehand if you are visiting throughout these times.

Kyoto experiences all the four seasons. Winter takes place in **December to February**, which is essentially pretty mild and averages **10°C**, but it's not uncommon for the temperature to go down below **0°C** by the month of **December**. **January** is normally the **coldest month** of the year.

From there, things start to limber up into spring in the months of **March to May**, with **March** getting the averages of **14°C**. **Spring starts** in earnest in the month of **April** and the temperatures just go up from there.

The months of **June to August** are the **summertime** when the average temperature plays around **28°C** which is the hottest month.

What you have to remember is that the month of **June** also marks the **beginning of rainy season** and it goes towards the end of the month. The **humidity** during this month can be extremely high.

The month of **September** marks as the **beginning of autumn** and it goes until early **November**. It gets very **rainy** so make sure you have your umbrella or raincoat ready. The temperature during these days begins to spill off going from the highs of summer down to **17°C**.

Regions at Glance

The popular districts of Kyoto include Gion and Arashiyama. Here is a short guide to Kyoto Districts including the attractions you will find in each of them.

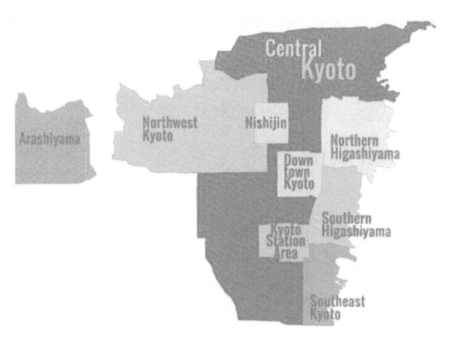

The districts in Kyoto precede the structure of the Kyoto ward. Theoretically every district in Kyoto must be a subarea of one Kyoto ward, but in fact, this isn't always the case. In common usage, a lot of people refer to an area as being part of a Kyoto District, when it essentially is part of the neighboring district.

Nishijin District

This neighborhood is the first one we visited it has fast become our favorite one. The Nishijin District is really quiet compared to Gion and Kyoto Station, and that's just one of the pleasant things about it. This district is also devised the Weaving district because you can find a lot of clothes factories here. The architecture here is also very remarkable, with well-preserved streets surrounded with wooden buildings that date back more than a century ago.

There are some really nice places to see while you are in this district. One is HOSOO, a groundbreaking textile company, factory, and showroom that feature designers that are using traditional materials to make them into modern, high-end interior design items. It is recommended to make an appointment before your intended visit. If you want to watch a kimono fashion show and shop a little bit, you may like to visit Nishijin Textile Center. If you want to have a little meal, there are some good places to eat while you are in Aishin-do.

Shinkyogoku District

If one of you plan of going to Kyoto is to do some shopping, that would be a really nice idea. This Shinkyogoku is the most popular place for shoppers, both locals and foreign. On this district, you will find unusual souvenirs, some of which you won't find anywhere else you go, but still very nice to have nevertheless. Walking down the Teramachi Street, you will find a more sophisticated shopping spot, one with fashion stores, art galleries, and bookstores. If you decide to go to the Imperial Palace, you would like going to the south along Teramachi Street and you will see the stores shift from boutiques to more consumer brands.

The Nishiki Market is also located here which is filled with busy locals shopping for their evening groceries and tourists try to taste some of the best traditional food the country has to offer. The market runs between Shinmachi and Teramachi and is a block north of Shijo.

Gion District

Gion is one of the most famous districts in the city and is located on the east side of the river. It's one of the main districts of Geisha and tourists are always visiting here in the evening hours to watch of the indefinable Maikos and Geikos. You can sign up for a Geisha-themed walking tour in town if you want to learn more things about the area. You will be fascinated with all the things you will discover during the visit, you will get to learn more about the teahouses and the history of the place.

It is amazing how quiet it is in this district compared to other districts like Shinkyogoku. You can simply look at one corner and it feels like you're in a private backyard. Thinking how popular Gion is with foreign visitors, it is nice to see that the neighborhood still remains very mysterious. A lot of streets in Gion are aimed for pedestrians that certainly cut out the traffic clamors you have to deal with in Shinkyogoku.

Northern Kyoto

This might be the best place to see temples and shrines. This is where Kinkakuji or Temple of the Golden Pavilion is located; you can also visit Ryoanji Temple and Ninnaji Temple. Other religious sites you can visit in this district are the Enryakuji and Daitokuji temples and the hot springs located at Kurama. You can visit the place for free but there is a small fee you need to pay if you want to get a tour inside the temple for about ¥ 500.

Just like other areas in the outskirts of Kyoto, you can simply spend a whole day here or just a couple of hours depending on your schedule and interests. When you walk Ninnaji to Ryoanji, you can find some local restaurants along the way if ever you get hungry. You can start your day at Arashiyama and then took the Keifuku Railways that's a local tram-like train, to Omuro Ninnaji Station.

Southern Kyoto

Fushimi Inari Shrine is Inari's main shrine and one of the most visited places in Kyoto. Inari is the god of rice and while the main shrine was constructed in the year 1499, the earliest constructions date back to 711. While the name might refer to a remarkable shrine, there are approximately 32,000 sub-shrines kept here too and if you like the idea of going to the top of the mountain, don't forget to bring a bottle of water with you. The main sub-shrines are all set along the path and there are also trails that commence in different directions in case you want to have a break from a busy crowd.

The trip takes approximately five minutes through train if leaving from Kyoto Station but the grounds could easily take a whole day. When you get to the place at least 9:00 AM or earlier, you'll be able to avoid the crowds and to enjoy the peace, not to mention, take better pictures.

Western Kyoto District

Arashiyama is one of the best most popular places in this district and is only a quick and cheap train ride away from the Kyoto Station. The most famous landmark, on the other hand, is Togetsukyo Bridge and is particularly popular during the fall season and when the cherry blossoms start to bloom. The best way to explore the area is by renting a bike and cruise at your own pace. If you want something more relaxing the cycling, then you may want to consider joining Hozu River Boat Tour or snag a ride on the Sagano Scenic Railway. If you are into history, you should spend some time in Saga-Toriimoto Preserved Street where you can see architecture from the Meiji Period.

There are people spend the entire day here strolling through the vibrant bamboo groves, the numerous temples, and other interesting places while others get their fill after a couple more hours. It is a good idea to choose what temples you would like to visit as they need a small entrance fee for admission and after a while that really starts to add up. From the top of Jojakkoji Temple, you have a nice view of downtown Kyoto.

Must Dos

Kyoto remains packed with remnants of its past glory as Japan's capital for more than a thousand years. Kyoto's spectacular collection of UNESCO World Heritage spots alone would be enough to make this city different from others, but Kyoto also has a still-working geisha district, some of the most wonderful cuisines of the country, and a whole lot of Zen. Not that it is all tradition and temples: the city also has its share of modern art and hip cafes and a touch of modern side of Japan. To make you experience the yin (the culture) and the yang (the modern) side of Kyoto, here is the list of the must do activities you may want to do when in traveling in this city.

1. Climb Up the Kyoto Tower and Have a 360° View of the City

KyotoTower

Standing 131 meters tall just in front of Kyoto Station, Kyoto Tower is the tallest building in the country and an uncommon modern iconic landmark in the city famous for its old shrines and temples. The tower was finished constructing in the year 1964, the same year as the opening of the Tokyo Olympics and the shinkansen.

There is a viewing deck placed 100 meters above ground where you can enjoy 360° view of Kyoto and to the extent that Osaka on clear days. Kyoto Tower stands over a typical commercial building that has restaurants, souvenir shops, a hotel, and a public bath located in the basement.

2. Have a Photo Op at Fushimi Inari Shrines

ToriGates

There are approximately 400 Shinto shrines in Kyoto, but Fushimi Shrines are unique and different from the others. Located on a forested hillside in the southern part of the city, Kyoto, Fushimi Inari is a 1,300-year-old temple devoted to Inari, the Shinto deity of sake and rice. This shrine complex was built in the 8th century, but it is not even the best thing about this place. Most of the visitors come for almost 10,000 red and orange lacquered Torii gates that are lined the 2.5-mile-long route up to Mount Inari, where the shrine is located. Sometimes in thick rows and other times more staggered, the gates are all inscribed with the names of Shinto disciples who contributed them.

Trekking up to the mountain takes about 3 hours and it can be slightly strenuous for some visitors. But there are many spots along the way where you can stop to take a bit rest.

3. Spend Your Afternoon Visiting Temples and Shrines

Spend your afternoon trying to explore and discover some of a fascinating cultural sites in Kyoto like sacred shrines, famous temples, and traditional houses of geisha. These stunning attractions will bring you to a different period in the history of Kyoto and provide you with a remarkable experience.

Kiyomizu-dera Temple   One of the easiest ways to do this is by joining a walking tour. The tour normally starts at the meeting point at Kyoto Station; you hop on a local bus going to Kiyomizu-dera Temple. Arriving at this World Heritage site, you must check out the main hall and then take a rest at wooden viewing deck that offers far-reaching views of Kyoto below.

After that, make a stop at Kōdai-ji Temple, where you could enjoy a 30-minute walk throughout the peaceful Zen gardens that limit one of the best Buddhist temples in the area. Then, head to Yasaka Shrine, which was founded more than 1,350 years ago.

4. Meander In and Wonder At the Bamboo Forest

Bamboo Forest   Submerge yourself in the picturesque beauty and historic landmarks of Arashiyama on this afternoon visit to one of most breathtaking districts of Kyoto. Stroll through a magical bamboo forest, meander the gardens of a 14th-century temple and get a glimpse of vibrant colored koi from the Togetsukyo Bridge. You could ride on a train going to the bamboo forest in Arashiyama. It is beautiful, dreamy, and extremely sustainable.

5. Join a Tea Ceremony

You need to join a tea ceremony and experience the traditional culture that surrounds green tea making while you are in Kyoto.

This is channeling your zen in the form of tea. The cleaning of the utensils, gently bowing your head as you receive your cup, and the three circular turns you take before taking a sip: it is not hard to see how intensely entrenched the slow and smooth movements of the tea ceremony are in Zen Buddhism. Sado or chado, as the ceremony is recognized, is in no way limited to Kyoto, but with the rich Zen connections of the city, it's a perfect place to experience it. Try to visit En, a little teahouse located in Gion with tatami tearooms and English-speaking Kimono-clad attendants. You will find it located beside Chionin Temple, just a short walk from the Chionmae bus stop on road number 206 from the Kyoto Station.

Right by the bamboo forestry, these gardens have lovely views back over the city and an attractively laid out traditional Japanese garden. The fee you are going to pay at the entrance includes a delicious Japanese biscuit and of course a nice cup of green tea.

6. Ride the Traditional Rickshaw

A man pulls a rickshaw down a narrow street in Kyoto   It's not common to see jinrikishas on most roads of Japan due to the number of today's vehicles. But in some popular historical tourist spots like Kyoto, jinrikishas are still offering attractions to the tourists, which include a special tour with the shafu or jinrikisha puller guiding you around. In the area close to Kiyomizu Temple, there are many very narrow paths like Nine-zaka, Kiyomizu-zaka, Nene-no-michi, and Sannen-zaka where you are able to hire and ride a jinrikisha.

A lot of residents of Kyoto have never ridden a jinrikisha themselves. But when you have ridden on one, you might agree that it would regret not experiencing it. Your eye level is going to be high and the ride will be fast, but extremely comfortable. You'll feel the breeze touches your face as your ride. This is a precious experience you wouldn't want to miss.

7. Feed the Snow Monkeys

When you visit Arashiyama, go up to the monkey park to interact with the monkeys and enjoy amazing views over the city of Kyoto. But be careful when feeding the money and make sure to treat them with respect as they can be wild.

SnowMonkeysatArashiyama

You can the money by your hand with they are in their enclosure. Just buy a bag of apple, peanuts, or chestnuts and hand them out to these majestic creatures. This is definitely a unique experience you will have in Kyoto.

8. Perform Meditation at the Ryoanji Temple

The Ryoanji Temple is a world heritage site popular for its simple scraped gravel rock garden. If you think the place is too

crowded for you, just walk around and you can find a nice bench in the garden by the Kyoyo-chi pond. It is picture perfect so you barely have to meditate to feel at peace, calm, and comfortable.

VisitorsmeditatingtheZengardenofRyoan-ji

9. Follow the Zen Monk Diet for a Day

If you are a vegetarian, then you might want to add vegetarian feast at the Kanga-an Temple in your itinerary.

The Chinese-style vegetarian or fucha ryori feast will exceed all your expectations. This might be the best meal you will have as it is extremely interesting. This might be a paradise for any vegetarians.

Dinner at Kanga-a Temple

A lot of Zen monks, who were not allowed to eat fish and meat, can still enjoy. So this type of cuisine was created to make dishes which looked like cooked seafood or raw fish and offered an extensive range of flavors to please their taste buds and eyes while letting the monks follow their vows.

Each of all 12 courses was carefully intended to be colorful, healthy, and delicious and it was all washed down with a nice drink like sake or sparkling sake drink known as Mio.

10.

Meet the Big Buddha

Bodhisattva Avalokiteshvara in Kyoto   Hello Kitty might be huge in the country, but Buddha is a lot bigger. Go to the 24-metre high statue of Bodhisattva Avalokiteshvara or the Bodhisattva of Mercy that was built in the year 1955 to honor the Japanese soldiers who died in World War II. There is a wishing ball here as well, so if you want to make a wish, maybe this place would make it comes to life.

11.

Play Dress Ups

Touristin kimonmosindfornictures There is no other way to completely engross yourself in Japan's cultures and traditions than dressing yourself up in a kimono while you are in Kyoto. So, this should definitely on your list of things you must do. It is the classic, clichéd Japanese image – the kimono-dressed woman holding a parasol, next to a branch of cherry blossom, a shrine, or a temple. But recreating the clichés is a lot of fun and something very meaningful.

Prepare yourself as you discover what it feels like to be famous and celebrity during a photo shoot. You can pose like a Japanese girl while enjoying the sights in the city for a day.

12. Have A Meet and Greet with Maiko

Meet and greet with a maiko at Kyoto tea house

If you don't like the idea of dressing up, then watch someone else dressed in their best attire. You can meet real Maiko and Geisha in Kyoto while sipping green tea and watching their stylish performance. You can go to a traditional Kyoto tea house and meet and have a conversation with them. Some of them can't speak English very well, but it's not a problem as there are in-house translators.

Doing this may cost you about ¥ 2500. This fee is for the show which comes with a supper of traditional local cuisine and you'll get everything that you pay for. It is believed that there are not more than a thousand geisha and maiko girls in the country, so it is a real privilege to actually meet them, enjoy watching their beautiful dancing and listen to their music.

13. Shop at Nishiki Market

Nishiki Market

The traditional market of Nishiki has a busy yet pleasant atmosphere that's really alluring to people who would like to explore the multiplicity of culinary treat that this city is known for. There are stores found all over the market comes in different sizes. Most of them specialize in a certain kind of food, and most things sold at the market is locally produced and made.

 A number of shops give out free samples to passing people that you can eat right on the spot. There are also some little restaurants and food booths that sell readymade food. Some are sitting down establishments, even though some have no more than a couple of stools. They normally specialize in one kind of food and are normally attached to stores that offer the same specialty.

14.

Relax at Onsens

Onsens are Japanese style hot springs where you can relax in even overnight. One of the most famous types is called rotten buro and has a natural setting outdoor bath. Visitors who want to hang out at one of these baths can enjoy the sights of surrounding cedar trees while they are getting rid of their pains and aches away.

An onsen in Kyoto

15.　Join Cooking Classes

A cooking class in Kyoto　If you love Japanese food, then you should definitely enroll yourself to a Japanese cooking class. The traditional cuisine of Japan is known to be fussy, has a demanding preparation, and complex ingredients. On a cooking course available in Kyoto, you will learn how to prepare a healthy Japanese lunch using simple ingredients which you can make for your friends and family once you come back home.

Day by Day Itineraries

No matter how long you're planning to stay in Kyoto, it's not very likely for you to see everything Kyoto has to offer, but by following the sample itinerary below, you'll be able to make the most of your trip to Kyoto. This is only a 3-day itinerary, but you can always modify it depending on your needs, preference, and schedule.

DAY 1: Temple Tours at Northwestern Kyoto

Morning

Kinkaku-Ji Temple

Zen Buddhist temple Kinkaku-Ji or also known as The Golden Pavilion is one of the most iconic temples in Japan so going here, you should expect to see a lot of other visitors wanting to take pictures and appreciate the beauty of the place. Avoid the huge crowd by arriving there early. Spending approximately 45 minutes here is enough for you to appreciate the real beauty of the place.

The place where Kinkaku-Ji is located was a private villa. In the year 1397, it was bought by Shogun Ashikaga Yoshimitsu, and, when he died, it was turned into a Zen temple by his son. In the mid-13th century, every complex saved for the pavilion was burnt to the ground. In the year 1950, the pavilion itself succumbed to flames set by a 22-year-old monk who tried to commit a suicide. As such, the pavilion that tourists enjoy these days was only established in the year 1955.

Ryoan-Ji Temple

From Kinkaku-Ji temple, you can just walk 20 minutes to Ryoan-Ji Temple. This is another Zen Temple as well as UNESCO World Heritage site. The garden of this temple is considered as one of the most excellent examples of a dry landscape garden, a form of Japanese Zen garden with huge rock formations on the top of little, smooth pebbles that have been lined up into well-ordered lines.

Kennin-Ji Temple

If you want to find a place that is more peaceful, then you may want to visit Kyoto's oldest temple, Kennin-Ji. Just like the Kinkaku-Ji, the place where Ryoan-Ji is located was in the 11th century a family estate. In the mid-13th century, a leader bought the land, constructed his home there, and established Ryoan-Ji. Like the Kinkaku-Ji, the temple was demolished throughout the Onin War, but the son of the leader reconstructed it in the late 13th century. The beautiful garden that you see today was established in the 18th century, by a garden specialist, Akisato Rito.

Afternoon

On Ryoan-Ji complex, you'll find a vegetarian restaurant called Seigeiin. They serve tofu and vegetables that are prepared in many different ways. They are not as healthy as what Zen Monks eat, but they are very delicious! One of the musts try foods here is

Okonomiyaki Katsu, which is a flavorful pancake cooked on a grill and topped with almost anything you want.

Ninna-Ji Temple

After eating your lunch, you can walk for another 20 minutes to get to Ninna-ji, which is the head temple of the Omuro School of the Shingon Sect of Buddhism. This establishment was founded in AD 888; Ninna-ji was also devastated by fire in the middle of Onin War. It was not until approximately 150 years later that it was reconstructed, and most of the things you can visit today are from 17th century. It has a very beautiful garden filled with cherry blossom during its season.

You have two options to choose from when going back to Kyoto. Riding the taxi which takes approximately 30 minutes is the easiest way, or if you want to save more money, then taking a bus would be a better option, this takes about 45 minutes to get to the Kyoto Station.

Arashiyama District

If you are not ready to end the day and relax in your hotel, you may still want to check out the Arashiyama district, which is one of most pleasant areas of Kyoto, mainly popular for the bamboo forest and the Tenryu-Ji Temple and named as UNESCO World Heritage. In order to get here, go to Kyoto Station and ride JR Sagano Line going to Arashiyama, this takes only 15 minutes and only cost ¥240. You can also take the Kyoto City bus #28 to take you there. Visit The Iwatayama Monkey Park to meet the red-faced monkeys. Make sure you have a bag of peanuts or bananas to feed them!

Evening

Have a nice dinner at any nearest izakaya or a Japanese-style pub and feast into plates of sashimi, tempura, and gyoza, with sufficient options to keep vegetarians from getting hungry. You can wash it all down with sake or nama biiru or their version of the beer.

DAY 2: Explore Nishiki Market, Gion, and the Higashiyama District

Morning

Nishiki Market

Start your day off by going to Nishiki Market. This market was first opened up in the early 14th century for buying wholesale fish products. Today, the enclosed arcade is lined with shops that sell all kinds of foods including souvenirs, tea, candy, as well as kitchen supplies.

A lot of shops offer free samples, so you'll never go wrong buying what you want for your breakfast. The finest restaurants you will find at Nishiki are not easily seen, there are a lot of shops hidden behind a lot of the seafood stalls that specialize in kaiseki and sashimi.

Nishiki Tenmangu

Don't forget to make a stop into the small but beautiful Nishiki Tenmangu shrine for a moment of serenity far from the hectic market.

Higashiyama and Gion

From Nishiki Market, go straight to Higashiyama and Gion. If there's still room for more food, then you may want to swing by department store basement food hall or what they locally called depachika at Takashimaya or Daimaru on the way going to Shijo Dori, one of the main east-west thoroughfares of Kyoto, across the Kamogawa.

Today, Gion is the most famous geisha district or hanamachi in Kyoto, but it was initially established for the visitors going to Yasaka Shrine, one of the most important Shinto shrines in the city. If you are swinging by around sunset, it's possible for you to see some geisha and maiko on the way to their evening appointments.

Afternoon

Spend the rest of the afternoon at Higashiyama district and visit Kiyomizu-Dera Temple, which is also a UNESCO World Heritage site. It gets steep as you walk up, you will pass by loads of restaurants and shops. A lot of shops have been selling on this place for years, catering to visitors.

Get this change to join a tea ceremony and enjoy a cup of matcha or their traditional, flavorful green tea.

Evening

Kiyomizudera

If ever you arrive early, you will have a chance to watch the sunset from Kiyomizudera. Kiyomizudera Buddhist Temple. The main hall of the temple offers a fantastic view of the vegetation underneath. You can explore the place by riding traditional rickshaw called jinrikishas.

At the main hall's base is the Otowa Waterfall. With the use of long poles with cups attached to it, visitors can drink water from one of the three streams, each of which is thought to carry a good luck.

You can end the day by walking through and having dinner at Gion. There are a lot of restaurants there that offer delicious authentic delicacies.

DAY 3: **The Last Day**

Last day is for relaxing.

Morning

Kimono Rental

Wake up early and go to the town to find where you can find a shop that will allow you to rent a kimono for the day. You can get crazy and wear it all day (make sure you return them before 5:00 PM!) or you can just stroll around for a few hours wearing it for beautiful pictures next to a cherry blossom tree or any iconic shrine of Kyoto.

Afternoon

Geisha and Maiko

Of course, you wouldn't want to miss meeting the geisha and maiko. Find a restaurant in the city where they show performances. After the performance, they are likely to join you at the table for a conversation while you are enjoying your lunch.

Afternoon

Onsen

Spend your afternoon relaxing at one of the city's tranquil onsens. These bath houses will definitely something you shouldn't miss on your last day. A nice onsen you can check out in the city is Funaoka Onsen, close to the Kuramaguchi train station. They have several different baths, which include a therapeutic one, a jet stream bath, a cold water plunge bath, outdoor baths, and even one with a mild current. The fee for the entrance costs ¥410.

Evening

Kyoto Tower

Of course, to end your tour, climb up the Kyoto Tower and get one last look at this beautiful city. If you have a fancy camera, take a photo and enjoy 360° sight of Kyoto at night.

Arriving in Kyoto

Kyoto is positioned near the center of Japan and the method of transport network makes it easily accessed from any international gateways. Kansai International Airport (KIX) is only more or less an hour away from Kyoto by land transport. Flight times to US West Coast and European destinations take just eleven hours, while Australia and Asia are even closer. Click on the table below to plan your route.

Closest International Airport

Kansai International Airport (KIX)		
JR Haruka Airport Express Train to Kyoto Station	75 min	JPY 2980
Shuttle Taxi to your hotel	95 min	JPY 3500
Limousine Bus to Kyoto Station	95 min	JPY 2300

Kansai International Airport (KIX)

Kansai International Airport positioned somewhat more than an hour away from Kyoto, is the most used international airport in Japan next to Tokyo. You can transfer from this airport to Kyoto station via JR Haruka express train, shuttle taxi straight to your hotel, or a limousine that you can hire from the airport.

Osaka Itami Airport (ITM)

Flights that are coming from Tokyo's airport, both Narita and Haneda, arrive at Itami airport once every hour. From Itami airport, ride a taxi or limousine going to your hotel or Kyoto station.

New Tokyo Narita International Airport (NRT)

If you're arriving at New Tokyo Narita International Airport (NRT) you'll be given with two options, you can travel by land or by air to the Kyoto area. The Narita Express or NEX train from Narita Airport takes around an hour to arrive at the Tokyo station, where the well-known bullet train or Shinkansen leaves. Riding Shinkansen to Kyoto Station is only 2 hours and 15 minutes. Flights from Narita going to Itami airport are about an hour long.

Central Japan International Airport (Centrair) (NGO)

Centrair is Japan's newest international airport established in the year 2005. It's only a quick 28 minutes going to the central part of Nagoya. And from Nagoya, it's only about 30 minutes to reach Kyoto.

Fukuoka Airport (FUK)

From Fukuoka airport, you can take the subway to Hakata Station that takes only 11 minutes, and transfer to Shinkansen. The Shinkansen arrives at Kyoto Station in not more than three hours.

Shuttle Taxi

If you are going to arrive off long-haul flights with hefty baggage, the taxi drivers will be more than happy to take you to your hotel from the airport to settle in. Normally, you share the taxi with up to nine other passengers who are going in the same direction of destinations. You can pre-book the trip online and pay it via credit card. The taxi ride takes a bit more than an hour depending on how heavy the traffic is and how far your destination is.

JR Haruka Airport Express Train

The JR Haruka express train takes only a bit more than an hour to reach Kyoto Station from the Kansai International Airport. The train is fast and quiet, where you can sit on big and comfortable seats, and offers enough space for luggage storage space. Destinations are usually announced in both English and Japanese.

Airport Limousine Bus

There are outstanding limousine services from both Kansai International Airport and Itami Airport that go to Kyoto Station. The trip going to Kyoto Station from KIX takes approximately 1 hour and 15 minutes, and from Itami approximately 55 minutes depending on how heavy the traffic is. The buses have plenty space for the luggage, the announcement is made in English, and you can make a reservation for the seat, or simply take the latest departure.

Shinkansen

Riding the Shinkansen bullet train is not simply traveling, but it's also a part of the Japan experience. The 510km trip from Tokyo to Kyoto is covered in a wonderful 2 hours and 15-minute trip. The trip shows you outstanding sights of Fuji, the highest mountain in the country, and the Pacific shoreline.

Getting Around

Kyoto is the most tourist-friendly city, with many road and street signs written in English and an easy-to-follow system of transportation. Here are types of transportation available in Kyoto:

Subway

Since Kyoto is comprised of many grid systems, navigating the city wouldn't be a problem for any visitors. However, underestimating distances will also be an easy thing to happen, so it is a good thing the local transport network covers every part of the city quite properly. It's easy to use Kyoto Subway Line, but it only has two lines: the first one is the inner city south-north Karasuma Line and the east-west Tozai Line, with intersection located at the station of Karasuma Oike.

Bus

The bus network, however, is a little bit more comprehensive. The green city buses you'll see around can take you around the most common spots of the city conveniently. The red buses, on the other hand, offer access to more remote parts of Kyoto.

If you want to go to some of the most popular attractions of the city, using the local train would be appropriate. You can buy passes at Kyoto City Bus and Subway Information Centers and automatic subway ticket vending machines.

You can use the Kansai Thru Pass for 2 or 3 days and offers unlimited travel on every subway and bus services around the city, while the City Bus All-day Pass offers unlimited travel on city buses within a central area drawn on the back of the pass.

Taxi

Kyoto has a lot of taxis, and it's easy to get into one in the center of the city. There are a lot of taxis that are waiting at Kyoto Station and they can also set tours for the best attractions around Kyoto.

Driving

Driving here isn't as intimidation as you might be expected as Japanese drivers, all in all, are generally disciplined and polite and as mentioned earlier, most road signs are translated into English. But you have to take note that parking can be very costly and traffic can heavy during rush house, so driving is something we wouldn't recommend.

Bicycle Hire

Riding a bicycle is very popular in Kyoto, and as a lot of city's major attractions in the city are located within cycling distance of the center of the city, it could be a convenient and satisfying way to get around.

Best Places to Stay

In Kyoto, you will never run out of places to stay. From cheap lodging house to five-star hotels, the city caters for visitors looking for a place to stay during their trip. Kyoto is full of ryokans or traditional Japanese inns, which makes it a nice place to try authentic Japan life. But you have to know that staying at nice ryokan can be costly and but it's definitely worth every cent you pay for it. Here are the accommodation options you have when staying in Kyoto.

Ryokans

If you ever want to stay in a ryokan for some extra interesting Japan stay, Kyoto is the best place to offer them. Some of the most foreign-friendly ryokans you will find are the following:

Tawaraya Ryokan

Address: Anenokoji-agaru, Fuyaco, Nakagyo-ki, Kyoto, Japan

Phone: +81 75-211-5566

Book here: www.ryokan.or.jp/english/yado/main/58900

Hiiragiya Ryokan

Address: Nakahakusancho, Fuyacho Anekoji-agaru, Nakagyo-Ku, Kyoto, Japan 604-8094

Phone: +81 75-221-1136

Book here: www.hiiragiya.co.jp/en/

Ryokan Shimizu

Address: 646-3 Kagiyacho (Wakamiyadori), Shimogyo Ward, Kyoto, Kyoto Prefecture 600-8317, Japan

Phone: +81 75-371-5538

Book here: www.kyoto-shimizu.net/eng/index.html

Hotels

Aside from wonderful Ryokans found in Kyoto, it also has a fantastic collection of hotels, which range from the most affordable ones to the five-star ones. Here are some of the affordable hotels you may want to check out:

First Cabin Kyoto Karasuma

Address: 〒 600-8099 331, Kamiyanagimachi, Bukkojidori Karasuma-higashiiru, Shimogyo-Ku, Kyoto-shi, Kyoto , takanohasukuea 4F

Phone: +81 75-361-1113

Book here: www.first-cabin.jp.e.jr.hp.transer.com/language/#en

Smile Hotel

Address: Japan, 〒 600-8494 Kyoto Prefecture, Kyoto, Shimogyo Ward 四条西洞院西入ル傘鉾町 59・61

Phone: +81 75-371-0941

Book here: www.smile-hotels.com/kyotoshijo/

Kyoto Garden Hotel

Address: Minamiiru, Oike, Muromachi-dori, Nakagyo-ku, Kyoto City, Kyoto, Japan

Phone: +81 75-255-2000

Book here: www.kyoto-gardenhotel.co.jp/en/

Business Hotels

Business hotels are basically cheaper hotels with small but enough rooms which offer everything you need during your accommodation. They are normally offering an outstanding value ideal for any travelers:

Eco and Tec Kyoto Hotel

Address: 40 Awataguchi Sanjobocho, Higashiyama Ward, Kyoto, Kyoto Prefecture 605-0035, Japan

Phone: +81 75-533-1001

Book here: www.ecoandtec.jp/en/

Sunroute Hotel Kyoto

Address: Japan, 〒600-8029 Kyoto Prefecture, Kyoto 下京区難波町 406

Phone: +81 75-371-3711

Book here: www.sunroute.jp/english/hotelinfo/kinki/kyoto/

Sakura Terrace the Gallery

Address: 39 Kamitonoda-cho Higashi-kujo Minami-ku Kyoto, 601-8002, JAPAN

Phone: +81 75-672-0002

Book here: www.sakuraterrace-gallery.jp/en/

Bed and Breakfast

Many locals turned their own houses into casual B&Bs. If you like the idea of staying somewhere with a local family and other visitors wanting to experience Kyoto, then this is the place for you. Hosts are normally very approachable and always willing to give you guides on where and how to go in a certain location for you to enjoy your trip:

B&B Juno

Address: 〒606-8417, 115-8 Jodoji Nishidacho, Sakyo Ward, Kyoto, Kyoto Prefecture 606-8417, Japan

Phone: +81 80-6104-5445

Book here: www.tripadvisor.com.ph/Hotel_Review-g298564-d634456-Reviews-B_B_Juno-Kyoto_Kyoto_Prefecture_Kinki.html

Guest House Keiko

Address: Japan, 〒604-0982 Kyoto Prefecture, Kyoto, Nakagyo Ward, 松本町 576-1

Phone: +81 80-6104-5445

Book here: www.guesthouse-keiko.jp/

Guest House Hennka

Address: 1-12 Imagumano Sozancho, Higashiyama Ward, Kyoto, Kyoto Prefecture 605-0955, Japan

Phone: +81 75-551-6229

Book here: www.rumbo.com/hotel/japan/-/kyoto/hotel-guest-house-hennka-kyoto.html

Ryokan Etiquette

Staying in a ryokan is an extraordinary experience, but there are several possible pitfalls a person who stays here the first time has to look out for. Here are some tips you must follow when staying at a ryokan:

Take Your Shoes Off

It's not surprising that a traditional hotel in Japan must follow the ancient practice of taking off shoes before entering a facility. A ryokan normally offers sleepers you can use inside. Taking your shoes off before entering is not optional, so make sure to follow this.

Indulge Your Tea

You will find packets of tea, teacups, a teapot, and perhaps some little snacks inside the room. These are free so you can have as much as you want. There will normally be a little table with cushions where you can sit around while enjoying your tea.

Keep Your Calm and Silence

A ryokan is normally considered to be a place to relax instead of being a place where you can just crash for the night. Make sure you keep your silence while you are around the facility. Refrain from stomping your feet while walking and talking on your phone too loud as this may disturb other guests who are trying to meditate or relax. But of course, this also applies to other types of accommodations.

Finding Your Bed

If it's your first time to stay at a ryokan, then it might be confusing for you to figure out if what's in front of you is a bed or a futon. Don't worry as the staff will come to your room to lay out futons for you. You might find this strange, but this is how it works. You don't have to give the person who prepares your bed as this can be seen offensive in the country on the whole.

Food and Drinks

Kyoto, in particular, is well-known for its tofu, kaiseki cuisine, as well as its Buddhist vegetarian fare. It is also a nice place to try other delicious Japanese cuisine. Here are the top 5 specialties of Kyoto and where you can try them:

Kyoto Style Sushi

The city of Kyoto prepares sushi a bit differently than other parts of Japan adding preserved fish and vinegary rice. The most common types of Kyoto-style sushi include *Sabazushi*, which has mackerel that is snugly wrapped around rice seized together with a thin sheet of kombu and *Hakozushi* is where the rice and fish are compelled into a wooden box-shaped mold normally incorporating grilled pike.

Where to eat: Izuju Sushi Restaurant

*Address:*Japan, 〒 605-0073 Kyoto Prefecture, Kyoto, Higashiyama Ward 祇園町北側２９２

Phone: +81 75-561-0019

Read more: https://en.yelp.com.ph/biz/ いづ重 - 京都市

Shojin Ryori

This is a Japanese Buddhist vegetarian cuisine and was developed from the strict diet of Buddhist monks. Forbidden from killing a life of other living creatures, Buddhist monks are only allowed to eat food that doesn't include meat and fish. Consisting of firmly vegetarian dishes, shojin ryori can nevertheless be flavorful and satisfying. Those who stay at ryokan can enjoy a meal as part of the stay.

Where to eat: Shigetsu

*Address:*Japan, 〒 616-0000 Kyoto Prefecture, Kyoto, Ukyo Ward, Sagatenryuji Susukinobabacho, 68

Phone: +81 75-882-9725

Read more: https://en.yelp.com.ph/biz/ 篩月 - 京都市

Tofu

Tofu is considered to be the bagel of Kyoto. This is definitely must try delicacy! Just like the vegetables, the way it is cooked has been improved, developed, and modified.

Where to eat: Tousuiro

Address: Japan, 〒 604-8001 Kyoto Prefecture, Kyoto, Nakagyo Ward 木屋町通三条上る上大阪町 517-3

Phone: +81 75-251-1600

Read *more: https://en.yelp.com.ph/biz/ 豆水楼 - 木屋町本店 - 京都市*

Vegetarian Soy Milk Ramen

This dish is entirely vegetarian but offers a strong flavor that will make you ask for more. The ramen noodles are made from molokheiya or Egyptian spinach and the soy milk makes its texture oh-so-creamy without empowering the taste of each ingredient used.

Where to eat: Mamazen in Kyoto

Address: Kyōto-fu, Kyōto-shi, Sakyō-ku, Shimogamo Higashitakagichō 13-4

Phone: +81 75-703-5731

Kyo-wagashi

Wagashi or the traditional Japanese sweets of Kyoto are usually served together with matcha or green tea. They also include red beans or anko and mochi.

Where to eat: Kagizen Yoshifusa

Address: 264 Gionmachi Kitagawa, Higashiyama Ward, Kyoto, Kyoto Prefecture, Japan

Phone: +81 75-561-1818

Read more: https://en.yelp.com.ph/biz/ 鍵善良房 - 本店 - 京都市

Need to Know

Kyoto is known to be a safe and nice place for tourists, with low crime rates and clean streets and surroundings. To be able to enjoy and make your stay even more enjoyable, here are things you need to know before your trip...

Customs and Etiquette

The Japanese are known in the world as polite and conservative individuals and even though there's a number of leeway for foreign visitors, following basic rules will make things go easily.

Greeting

Japanese bow their heads when they greet people, the lower the bow is, the bigger respect is shown. It's also important to remove your shoes when entering a shrine, temple, and sometimes, even restaurants, especially the more traditional ones.

Tipping

All travel guides remind this: DO NOT TIP. No matter what the situation is, tipping isn't needed anywhere in Japan. They may find it rude and offensive. Although there is few high-end traditional ryokan where some guests give a little tip to the staff or manager. But again, this is not necessary. You shouldn't feel bad about not giving a tip to the hard working servers at restaurants either as they include a service charge of 10% to 15% in your total bill.

Bath Time

If ever you'll have the chance to try bathing at a traditional Japanese bath at a public bathhouse, hot spring, or even ryokan, the last thing you want to do is to get the water dirty. Make sure that you use the separate wash area when showering and then properly before you get into the big common bathtub. And don't forget to be modest and change and get dressed in private.

Money

The Japanese Yen (JPY = ¥) is the currency used by Japan.

Notes: ¥10,000; ¥5,000; ¥2,000; ¥1,000

Coins: ¥500; ¥100; ¥50; ¥10; ¥5y; ¥1

To find the best exchange rate, it's best to go to the bank, but if you don't want to bother going to the bank in the middle of your trip, changing your home currency at the airport would be a smart thing to do.

It is also easy to find an ATM machine if ever you need to cash out some money, though credit cards aren't as commonly used as in the United States. On expense, Kyoto is just like Tokyo in terms of hotels, restaurants, street foods, and transportations.

Internet / Wi-Fi

For all the technological advancements of Japan, there's still a relative lack of public places to get connected online. Though most business hotels or modern Western-style hotels will have either free LAN or Wi-Fi access to the room or the lobby, the more traditional Japanese hotels are not likely to have anything more than a one shared computer in the lobby. But if your hotel doesn't offer the internet, it's easy to go to coffee shops to get connected. There's also free Internet access available at the Kyoto International Community House located on Sanjo-dori, while the smart tourist information office in the station also has some Internet-connected computers available at ¥100 per ten minutes. You can get a fuller list of places around the city where you can get connected to the internet from an English-speaking staff there.

Street and Road Signs

As mentioned earlier, getting around Kyoto is easier than other parts of Japan as most of their signs are translated into English. On the streets, in train stations and even the restaurant menus are available in English for the convenience of the tourists.

No Trash Bins

This comes as surprising because of the fact that Kyoto or Japan, on the whole, is a very clean place, but one thing you'll notice is that trash bins are not easily spotted. Walking through a city as big as Kyoto, bins are almost one hour apart from each other, so make sure you always have a space in your bag for trash.

Fast facts

Population: 1.5 million
Spoken languages: Japanese, minimal English

Electrical: 110 Volts, 60 Hertz
Phone/calling code: + 81 75

Safety Information

Though Kyoto is one of the safest places among Japanese big cities or anywhere in the world, sometimes an emergency occurs inevitably.

119 is the direct-dial free phone number for non-criminal emergencies Simultaneous telephone interpretation service is provided in five languages.

General Tip:

It's extremely important to take basic safety measures. Keep your valuables at the hotel's front desk or in the room's safe is there's any. You might also want to keep the original copies of your travel documents and bring a copy of them if you are going out, especially your passport. Don't forget to attain travel and health insurance, and please don't forget to pack enough medication to last the duration of your stay. It might also be a nice idea to register with the embassy of your home country before leaving the country.

Emergency Hospital

Japanese Red Cross Kyoto Daini Hospital: 075-231-5171
University Hospital, Kyoto Prefectural University of Medicine: 075-251-5111
Kyoto University Hospital: 075-751-3111
Japanese Red Cross Kyoto Daiichi Hospital: 075-561-1121
Misugikai Medical Corporation Otokoyama Hospital: 075-983-0001
National Hospital Organization Kyoto Medical Center: 075-641-9161Meiji
University of Integrative Medicine Hospital: 0771-72-1221

Medical Services

If ever you become ill while you are on your Kyoto trip, you can easily buy medical supplies at local drugstores. You can find a lot of hospitals in Tokyo, ranging from small clinics to big institutes. Credit cards are hardly accepted at Japanese pharmacies and hospitals. If you have insurance for medical care, get a list of acceptable international hospitals from your insurance company. In a lot of cases, you insurance will cover your hospital expenses.

Police Box System or Koban

Koban is the operated police boxes found in most Japanese neighborhoods. They normally have red lights and the signs are written in English. If you have to ask for directions, use the lost and found service, got robbed, or want to make a report for any crime, you have to go to Koban. In most tourist destinations, they're likely to have an English-speaking staff officer. If ever there's no English-speaking officer is available, they normally have an interpreter. You have to know that they are not always available for 24 hours. However, you can reach the police whenever by calling 110 or the local numbers listed below:

Kawabata-police station: 075-771-0110
Kamigyo-police station: 075-465-0110
Higashiyama-police station: 075-525-0110
Horikawa-police station: 075-823-0110
Shimogyo-police station: 075-352-0110
Shimogamo-police station: 075-703-0110
Fushimi-police station: 075-602-0110
Yamashina-police station: 075-575-0110
Ukyo-police station: 075-865-0110
Minami-police station: 075-682-0110
Kita-police station: 075-493-0110
Nishikyo-police station: 075-391-0110

Non-Criminal Emergencies

119

If you have a non-crime related emergency you want to report, then this number is what you should call. Some of the situations you can call these numbers are fire and medical emergencies. This is also used all over the country. The city of Kyoto offers a concurrent telephone interpretation service available in five languages which are English, Portuguese, Spanish, Korean, and Chinese, to help foreign visitors who need help.

Using 119 Emergency Number

1. Dial 119 on any phone.
*The call is free of charge from public and mobile phones.
2. Describe what has happened clearly.
3. Give the most important information like location, address, and anything the operator asks you.

Maps You Need

Places

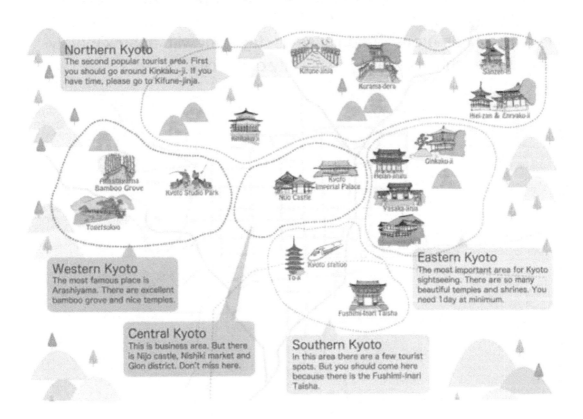

Kyoto is one of the most popular cities in Japan and with the number of attractions and things to do in this city, this does not really come as a surprise. But even though it's one of the top destinations in Japan for tourists, it does well in preserving the real beauty of its rich culture and history, being the only big city in Japan to escape the destruction caused by the World War II. Well-known as the home to the emperor and the main cultural center of Japan for more than a thousand years, Kyoto at present boasts various great examples of paintings, sculptures, and other forms of arts in its numerous galleries and museums. In Kyoto, you will also find centuries-old structural designs, which mostly influenced by Buddhism and found in well-kept temples. Kyoto stays to play a significant role in the religion of Japan, with 30 of the temples in the city still serving as centers of numerous Buddhist sects, together with approximately 200 Shinto shrines within the vicinity of the city.

1. Fushimi Inari-Taisha Shrine

If you have seen or read the film or novel 'Memoirs of a Geisha' by Arthur Golden and liked it, then you would love to see this place. While here you can reenact the scene where young Chiyo runs through endless rows of bright red Torii gates in your mind while seeing them in person. While most of the scenes in the movie were shot in California, there are a few scenes that are filmed in Kyoto and Fushimi Inari-Taisha Shrine was one of the locations of the film.

Fushimi Inari is the most important of many shrines dedicated to Inari, the Shinto god of rice. It is believed that foxes are the messengers of Inari, which is the reason why there are a lot of fox statues throughout the shrine vicinity. Fushimi Inari Shrine has old origins, preceding the moving of the capital to Kyoto in 794.

Address68 Fukakusa Yabunouchicho, Fushimi Ward, Kyoto, Kyoto Prefecture 612-0882 Japan **Phone#** 81 75-641-7331 The most surprising and a unique thing about this shrine is the great number of Torii gates in different sizes, assembled in myriad rows. It's estimated that there are well more than 10,000 Torii gates at Fushimi Inari-Taisha Shrine. I bet you didn't expect it to be that much! They form roofed trails going up the mountain and you can walk for hours under this charming roof.

Every Torri gate has a black writing with the name of the company which donated it to the shrine. Inari is known to be the god of rice, but as well as the patron of business and having a Torii gate here is thought to carry good luck. There are also some that have Latin inscriptions written on them. And just like most shrines in Japan, the entrance here is free.

2. Kyoto Station Building

All of the major cities of Japan have a main central station, offering a focus point for business and the everyday activities of the people who live in the city, and in a lot of cases, offering a cultural blend from which the cities themselves have developed.

Kyoto station building is the main hub of Kyoto's public transportation. In this station building, you will find a department store, a shopping mall, a theater, a hotel, restaurants, and other facilities that you can enjoy. The Kyoto Tourist Information Center is located on the building's second floor. Here you can get a free Kyoto City Bus Travel map, Kyoto City Map, as well as other information that will help you have an easier and hassle free trip in Kyoto.

 Having the Kyoto Station Building and the neighboring blocks, the Kyoto Station Area is not precisely a tourist's destination, but chances are, you will end up spending a lot of time here. The shinkansen or bullet train, the Haruka airport express train and some other train lines all operating out of the Kyoto Station, which means you will most likely most likely arrive here.

Address: Higashishiokoj Kamadonocho,Shimogyo Ward, Kyoto, Kyoto Prefecture Japan For those who have a soft spot for unique architecture, the Kyoto Station complex offers an enticingly wonderful facility that balances the ancient and traditional buildings of the history of Kyoto, with a design that fascinates architects from a different part of the world.

The sight of Kyoto from the train platforms is pretty unattractive – you'll see many concrete, neon, and unpleasant billboards. But, taking the time to explore the place will surely make you enjoy your time. When getting out of the city, you will find the beauty you have come in search of.

The main things to do here are shopping in the big malls and electronics emporiums inside and around the station or going to the three of the massive temples that are located within the station.

3. Kinkaku-Ji Temple or The Golden Pavilion

Kinkaku-Ji Temple or also known as The Golden Pavilion stands in front of Kyoko-chi pond. The pavilion and its clear reflection on the water along with isles and trees pile into an exquisiteness and produce a peaceful setting. This Zen temple signifies Kitayama-bunka, colorful culture that was a combination of new samurai culture and traditional aristocratic culture.

This UNESCO World Heritage Site is selected as a national special landscape and a national special historic site. This is one of the most famous and one of the best places to visit when you are in Japan.

Address1 Kinkakujicho, Kita Ward, Kyoto, Kyoto Prefecture 603-8361, Japan **Phone:** 81 75 461 0013 The pavilion has Buddha relics and every floor has a unique architectural theme. The image of the temple opulently decorated in gold leaf replicates attractively in the water of Kyokochi, the mirror pond. The garden of the temple is also a picturesque delight and has in its grounds a pleasant teahouse.

It's possibly the most widely-recognized attraction in Kyoto. Seen replicated in the adjacent "mirror pond" with its small islands of pine and rocks.

The first purpose of the building was to serve to be the home of the retiring Shogun Ashikaga Yoshimitsu. The gold-leaf-decorated building was eventually turned into a Zen temple just after his death. In 1950, the temple was burned by a 21-year-old monk. The temple was reconstructed five years lave and continues to function as a house for sacred relics.

4. Ginkaku-Ji Temple or The Silver Pavilion

The Rinzai-shu sect Zen temple signifies Higashiyama-bunka, a nation of Wabi and Sabi. This simple culture is pretty opposing with flashy Kitayama-bunka, a nation that is signified by Kinkaku.

Ginkaku or the Silver Pavilion and Togu-do buildings are national treasures. The garden is labeled as a national special landscape.

The Silver Pavilion was constructed to follow the model of the Golden Pavilion. And the gardens of the temple are some of the best things in Japan. The place is so peaceful and relaxing and stimulated pleasing feelings.

The sand garden at Ginkaku-Ji and the mountain of sand that represents Mount Fuji are quite a view and the moss covered forested grounds are also remarkable.

Address: 2 Ginkakujicho, Sakyo Ward, Kyoto, Kyoto Prefecture 606-8402, Japan Phone: +81 75-771-5725 A first look of the Silver Pavilion can be relished as soon as you enter the grounds. Formally known as Kannonden or Kannon Hall, the two stories of the pavilion are built in two different construction styles and have a Kannon statue, the Buddhist goddess of mercy. But people can't enter inside the pavilion.

Unlike the Golden Pavilion which is color yellow/gold where its name based on, the Silver Pavilion was never covered in the color that comes with its name. Instead, it's thought that the name arose as a nickname over a century after the construction of the building to match with the Golden Pavilion. On the other hand, it's explained that moonlight reflecting on the dark exterior of the building gave it a silvery look.

5. Toei Uzumasa Eigamura or Kyoto Studio Park

The Toei Uzumasa Eigamura also called Kyoto Studio Park or Movie Land by tourists, is a film set which is also a theme park. Basically, this is a small town from the Edo Period, the park boasts a collection of different traditional buildings which are sometimes used as a background for shooting historical films and TV shows.

The park has the whole streets portraying town scenes, which include an imitation of the old Nihonbashi Bridge, a Meiji Period police box, a customary courthouse, and a few parts of the old Yoshiwara red light district. Park employees are wearing historic outfits add to the town's atmosphere. The actual filming takes place intermittently in different parts of the park, and visitors can watch the shooting.

Address10 UzumasaHigashihachiokacho,Ukyo Ward, Kyoto, Kyoto Prefecture616-8161, Japan **Phone**+81 75-864-7716

Eigamura also has some other amusements and attractions for guests to experience which include a ninja maze, ninja performances, a 360 degree 3D theater, filming demos, and a haunted house that is known to be one of the scariest in the country. Some of these may require you to pay an additional entrance fee. There are also shows about the famous video arcades, TV series, restaurants, games, and souvenir stores.

You can also dress up in the ancient outfit and get your photo taken wearing more than 30 different costumes including geisha, samurai, and ninja. You can also wear these costumes while you are exploring the park.

6. Nijo-jo Castle

Address541 Nijojocho,Nakagyo Ward, Kyoto, Kyoto Prefecture 604-8301,Japan **Phone**+81 75-841-0096

With gigantic stone walls bounded by deep moats, Nijo-jo Castle fully shows the power that the Shoguns or the military warlords exerted over the country for much of its history. Unlike the more popular Himeji-jo Castle in Himeji, which ascends upward, somewhat in the method of European castles, Nijo-jo Castle is considered by low but nevertheless impressive and grand constructions, all of which are walled by stunning gardens. You are able to enter the Ninomaru Palace, which is well-known for its "nightingale floors." The pretty carvings and panels here reflect the huge power and approaches of the warlords who lived the castle. After exploring the Ninomaru Palace, take a relaxing walk through the magnificent Seiryu-en Garden, which frames the buildings of the castle.

The only problem about going here is it always packed with people who also want to see this beautiful place. So, if you want to see this place while there are still not many people around, make sure that you come early, just right after it opens up for public.

Their main attractions of the castle are the building of Ninomaru-Goten building and one of its three gardens. Ninomaru-Goten, a national treasure, are a traditional samurai housing architecture. Shoheki-ga paintings in the building were made by Kano Tanyu and his company. Ninomaru teien has a wonderful characteristic unusual to garden design in the early Edo days

Ninomaru Goten mansion is considered to be a national treasure. Ninomaru Teien garden is selected as a national special landscape.

7. Gion District

Gion is one of the most popular and most exclusive geisha districts in the entire country. It recently went through a renovation project and all tools were moved underground.

Gion is the setting of the film 'Memoirs of a Geisha' and there are guided tours organized around it that show curious guests the places written in the book. But most people's favorite remains to be the walking tour wearing traditional kimono, which is a wonderful chance for cultural immersion while discovering the drenched in history streets of Gion.

Address 23-1 Nagitsuji Fushikawacho, Yamashina Ward, □□□
□□□ Kyoto Prefecture 607-8167, Japan **Phone** +81 75-591-6602 But Gion is even more interesting during the evening. The old wooden teahouses make the guests feel welcome, and geiko and maiko entertain visitors as ever. But this is a cultural experience a lot of foreigners find intimidating. And as a matter of fact, it would be a shame to miss. At Gion Hatanaka Cultural Center you can find a graceful maiko performance while trying the delicious local delicacies. This is such a wonderful experience and an exceptional chance to have your photo taken with a gorgeous maiko!

Now, if you walk around the streets of Gion long enough you can still see some geisha walking by. Some people stop them for a picture or two. Don't take a picture of them without permission as this is considered very rude and obnoxious.

8. Kiyomizu-Dera Temple

Kiyomizu-Dera is yet another UNESCO Heritage Site you can find in the beautiful city of Kyoto. The biggest attraction you will find here is the main hall, which is made completely out of wood, meaning only literally woods! You cannot find a single nail used to build the hall and you'll be stunned at the craftsmanship used to it.

The hall is constructed over a cliff and its big veranda is reinforced by some really tall pillars. On top of having remarkable views over the city and the waterfall close to it, its architecture is truly unique.

Address 294 Kiyomizu 1-chome, Higashiyama Ward, Kyoto, Kyoto Prefecture 605-0862, Japan **Phone** +81 75-551-1234 Back in the period of Edo period people believed that whoever jumped from the 13-meter high cliff and survived, would get their wish granted. The record shows that more than 200 people jumped and only over 85% of them survived. This practice is today banned for apparent reasons.

But if you want to try your luck, you can still give the Two Stones a shot. The Love Stones are the two stones 6 meters apart from each other and whoever manages to walk between them while their eyes are closed are going to find love.

You can go to Kiyomizu-Dera Temple by yourself or you can join a little tour group led by a scholar who will set the new light on the different Japanese religious ceremonies and rituals. Some people are not into tours, but it would be nice to have some explains to you the history of a certain place. Plus, this specific tour includes some other temples and shrines.

9. Ryoanji Temple or Temple of the Dragon at Peace

Ryoanji, also known as the Temple of the Dragon at Peace, has one of the best rock gardens you will find in the country. On the top of this, it is also a UNESCO Heritage Site. You can also meditate from the porch, which was actually a pretty nice thing to do while enjoying the warm autumn sun. The grounds have numerous details to be explored and a huge pond covered with pretty water lilies.

Anyone can enter the temple building, as long as you don't forget to take your shoes off. But the rock garden is the best thing to finding here and can either leave you cold or stir the deepest revelation inside you.

Address13 Ryoanji Goryonoshitacho,Ukyo Ward, Kyoto, Kyoto Prefecture616-8001 Japan Phone+81 75-463-2216 The temple grounds of Ryoanji also have a quite large park area with pond, situated underneath the main buildings of the temple. The pond was established at the time when the site still served as a villa of an aristocrat and features a little shrine on one of its three little islands you can enter over a bridge.

On the top of that, some beautiful walking trails, the park also offers an eating place which specializes in the specialty of Kyoto, which is Yudofu or boiled tofu. The food is served in beautiful tatami rooms that look out onto a customary Japanese garden.

10.   Kyoto Gosho or Kyoto Imperial Palace

Kyoto Gosho or Kyoto Imperial Palace keeps the form of Kyoto's original palace.

Located in the middle of the expansive Kyoto Imperial Palace Park, the Kyoto Imperial Palace is an enclosed compound where you can find some extravagant buildings constructed in the traditional Japanese style. If you are expecting a European-style palace, you may be amazed to see the low rooflines and wooden building of the Kyoto Imperial Palace.

Address: Kyotogyoen, Kamigyo Ward, Kyoto, Kyoto Prefecture602-0881 Japan Phone:+81 75-211-1215

Those who visit can explore the grounds by themselves, and reservation and joining a tour is not necessary anymore. The palace is open from Tuesday to Saturday and closed on Sunday and Monday.

Next to the Imperial Palace are some other historic sites are situated within Kyoto Imperial Park, like Sento Palace. The admission to the Sento Palace will still need early reservations and join a tour, and the tours are done twice to five times a day.

11. Arashiyama Bamboo Grove

You can't leave Kyoto without walking in the middle of these tall bamboo groves. While Arashiyama isn't exactly located in Kyoto but instead in a region on the outskirts of the city, it's still easily accessible by train and a certainly a must-see attraction.

Address:Ukyo Ward, Kyoto, Kyoto Prefecture Japan   The best and easiest way to travel around this area is to rent a bicycle, which isavailable for about ¥1000 close to the train stations. Cycling through rustic residential regions and past fields while you travel between temples could be one of the most fun parts of going to Arashiyama. There's also a beautiful well-kept town area close to the Adashino Nenbutsuji Temple.

Arashiyama becomes most beautiful around the early part of April and the second half of the month of November when the cherry blossom and fall color seasons normally is at its peak. Throughout the summer months, traditional cormorant fishing is practiced on the Hozu River for visitors to watch. Another good time to go here is during the Hanatoro illumination in December when lanterns line the streets and bamboo groves.

12.　　Heian-Jingu Shrine

Heian-Jingu was established in the year 1895 to honor the 1100th anniversary of the foundation of Kyoto as Japan's capital. The pretty new shrine has interesting halls and good-looking gardens. The main halls characterize 5/8 scale imitations of the first Imperial Palace constructed in Heian-Kyo in 794 and carry the atmosphere of the style of the Heian period.

Outside the shrine and curving over a hectic road is the torii gate of Heian Jingu, the leading found in Japan. Constructed in the year 1929, it's 24.2 meters high; the top rail is 33.9 meters long.

Address Okazaki Nishitennocho, Sakyo Ward, Kyoto, Kyoto Prefecture 606-8341, Japan **Phone** +81 75-761-0221 The green, orange, and white buildings of Heian Jingu are planned to imitate of the old Kyoto Imperial Palace that was ruined in the year 1227, at two-thirds the original size. The main buildings are the distinguished East Hon-den and West Hon-den, and the Daigoku-den, wherein the Heian emperor would issue rulings.

You can find three stroll gardens at Heian Jingu, located east, west, and north of the shrine itself. They follow the Heian aesthetic of directing on a great pond, which is an unusual feature at a Shinto shrine. The foothold path that crosses the water is made from the columns of a 16th-century bridge that crossed the Kamo-gawa before an earthquake ruined it.

Shinen Garden, which arrives on the left when you're facing the main hall, shouldn't be missed. Typical of gardens built during the

Meiji Era, it is well-known for its howling cherry trees in spring, its irises and water lilies during the summer, and its changing maple leaves during the fall.

13.   Sanjūsangen-dō Temple

The remarkable Sanjusangendo Temple of Kyoto, established in the 12th-century, where you can find 1001 carved wooden statues of Kannon – the Buddhist Goddess of Mercy – position in ranks in the main hall: 500, in ten rows of 50, on every side of the sat figure of Senju Kannon. Sanjusangendo is the only such Sentai Kannon-do left in existence. The 1001 images are about 167-centimeter tall and were made using a method known as yosegi, which allowed numerous craftsmen to work on a single statue. First, hollow blocks of wood were put together and coarsely carved, and then the images were excellently engraved and lacquered for good preservation.

Address 657 Sanjusangendomawari, Higashiyama Ward, Kyoto, Kyoto Prefecture 605-0941, Japan **Phone** +81 75-561- Every 15th day of January, every year, an archery competition, called kyudo, is held outside the hall. This ceremonial is done on the west side of the hall and includes shooting an arrow 60 meters at a 1-meter diameter target. As the arrows appear to shoot through the hall the ceremony is called Toshi-ya. The event started in the Edo Period and was popular among the samurai of the time.

The name of the temple literally means "hall (do) with thirty-three (sanjusan) spaces between the columns (gen)."

Sanjusangendo Temple is 64-meter long and 13-meter wide and is formally known as Rengeoin Temple or Lotus King. Sanjusangendo was built on the orders of ex-Emperor Goshirakawa in 1164 with support from Taira-no-Kiyomori, the de-facto military monarch at that time. But the original building was ruined by fire in the year 1249 and reconstructed in the year 1266.

14.   To-Ji Temple

To-ji or also known as the East Temple was established together with Sai-Ji, the West Temple, in 794 when Kyoto was made as Japan's capital. These two temples were intended to guard the city but Sai-Ji destroyed after a fire in 990.

Kondo hall, the five-storied pagodas, Renge-mon and Daishi-do hall gate are national treasures.

The pagoda of To-Ji Temple stands above the suburban stretch of southern Kyoto, guaranteeing the visitor that there is still the plenteously amount of beauty left in the city.

Address: Kujocho, Minami Ward, Kyoto, Kyoto Prefecture601-8473 Japan Phone: +81 75-691-3325 As you enter Kyoto from the south or west, you may find fall into misery as you approach Kyoto and find yourself bounded by a drab span of sloppy apartments and garish signs common in most cities in Japanese. Just as you are starting to think you have been had, you will see the rising point of To-ji Temple's pagoda standing above the sprawl to the southwest part of the station. This will set your mind comfortable and inspire you to explore the city more.

While you could walk there in approximately 15 minutes from Kyoto Station, it is not a mainly easy walk, so it is better to hop on a local on the Kintetsu line from Kyoto Station and ride it a stop to To-Ji Station, from which the temple is a short walking distance. No matter what you do, if you are in the city on the 21st of any month, don't miss the Kobo-san Market, held on the temple grounds.

15.   Nanzen-Ji Temple

Nanzen-Ji Temple is one of the best temples you will find in the Northern Higashiyama district. This temple is an extensive Zen paradise bounded by opulent green hills.

Address: Japan, 〒606-8435 Kyoto Prefecture, Kyoto 南禅寺福地町86
Phone: +81 75-771-0365 Nanzen-Ji, one of the large Zen temples in Kyoto once was the highest ranked Zen temple in the country. Ko-Hojo and O-Hojo buildings are national treasures. Fusuma-e paintings in the two buildings were created by Kano Eitoku, Kano Tanyu, and Kano Motonobu. The Zen temple is also well-known for its Karesansui garden that is thought to have been laid out by Kobori Enshu.

You can find every element there: the remarkable San-Mon gate, the delicate karesansui garden, the spacious main hall, and large footpaths that invite meditative walking. Most of all, the main compound is fenced by small but outstanding sub-temples, each of which is worth visiting. These include Nanzen-in, Konchi-in, and the often-unnoticed Tenju-an. But for us, personally, Nanzen-Ji is Nanzen Oku-no-in, a waterfall grotto approximately 200 meters up in the hills at the back of the temple is the best part of this place. For you to get there, walk under the brick aqueduct and take a hard left and follow the small stream. Look on the top of the waterfall and you will find a little grotto hidden in a big boulder that has some interesting Buddhist images.

16. Nishi Honganji Temple

Nishi Honganji Temple is the main temple of the original Jodo-Shinshu sect. This is an exceptional example of Buddhist architecture. Tourist attractions include the Hondo or Main Hall, reconstructed in the year 1760 with numerous fine rooms ornamented with paintings on gold backgrounds and several important statues, some dating back from the 6th century. Also of interest is the Founder's Hall with its much-respected statue of Shinran, carved in the year 1244 and later protected with a coat of lacquer blended with his ashes.

Address Japan, 〒600-8358 Kyoto Prefecture, Kyoto, Shimogyo Ward 堀川通花屋町下ル Phone +81 75-371-5181 Another remarkable building is the Daishoin, or Treasury, with numerous rooms named after the beautiful ceiling and wall paintings with which they are decorated, which include the Sparrow Room, the Room of the Wild Geese, and the Chrysanthemum Room with its fine 17th-century paintings of flowers in gold and white by Kaiho Yusetsu. Also of interest is the Higashi-Honganji Temple of the Jodo-Shinshu sect, established in the year 1602 and home to numerous examples of fine artwork.

Useful Tip: Just some parts of these temples are accessible to the public, so make sure to make arrangements earlier of your visit to include other areas not usually open to the public.

17.   The Kyoto National Museum

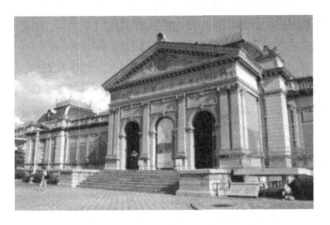

Along with the numerous fine old temples with their important artworks, Kyoto also boasts numerous remarkable collections in its various world-class museums and galleries. Maybe the most popular are the National Museum, an art gallery developed in the year 1897 that is extensively considered the most important such museum in the country. Focusing mainly on pre-modern Asian art, mainly examples from Japan, and the museum was totally renovated in the year 2014 and boasts many examples of remarkable art and applied arts spread throughout numerous buildings. Also worth seeing is Kyoto Municipal Museum of Art, established in the year 1928 and featuring most significant works by Takeuchi Seihō, one of leading artists of the 20th century of Japan.

Address527 Chayacho,HigashiyamaWard, Kyoto, Kyoto Prefecture605-0931, Japan Phone +81 75 525 2473 The permanent collection of the museum is presented to the public in rotating displays and has a wide diversity of cultural properties, which includes archaeological sculptures, relics, ceramics, costumes, calligraphy, and paintings. It's housed in the roomy galleries of the Heisei Chishinkan, a building created by Taniguchi Yoshio and opened in the year 2014. The architect is also known for the Horyuji Homotsukan at the Tokyo National Museum, the Mimoca Art Museum in Marugame, the Sea

Life Aquarium at Tokyo's Kasai Rinkai Park, and his redesign of the Museum of Modern Art in New York.

Along with the enduring exhibitions, temporary special exhibitions are held in the original main building of the museum that was built during the Meiji Period in the year 1895. Renamed the Meiji Kotokan, the redbrick building, along with the equally styled main entrance gates, are gorgeous examples of Meiji architecture and have been labeled as important cultural properties.

18.   Katsura Imperial Villa

Address Katsuramisono Nishikyo Ward, Kyoto, Kyoto Prefecture 615-8014, Japan Phone +81 75-211-1215

The Katsura Imperial Villa was originally built in the year 1624 for Prince Hachijo Toshihito, brother of Emperor Goyozei, and is home to one of most well-known historic gardens in the country. Designed by Kobori Enshu with the assistance of the prince, this spectacular garden is located in such a way that the guests constantly sees things from the front; smaller gardens are assembled around a large pool with the peaks of Mounts Arashiyama and Kameyama in the background. The highlights in the area include the Miyuki-mon Gates and several garden paths, some made from river gravels and others of four-sided cobbles, enclosed by mosses and bushes, and will lead you through further gates into the garden inside with a group of buildings known as the Goten at its center. A particular highlight here is the porch of Furu-shoin, mainly designed to let observation of the moon, and the three rooms of the Naka-shoin with its frequent fine paintings by the most important artists of the country.

You can only see the villa by joining the tours held by the Imperial Household Agency. They last about an hour and are in Japanese only, but there is an English audio guide available as well. Throughout the tour, the tour group walks along the circular walking trail of the garden around the central pond. You can see the palace buildings only from the outside. You can take photos from some selected spots.

The Katsura is very successful because it's a universal work of art, on the whole, one wherein everyone can see something to admire and enjoy. Though it's big, it seems more like an assortment of modest experiences than an expansive villa. Though minimal, it has a sophistication that gives it elegance. Despite its age, it was well maintained and seems like new. You can't find other Japanese artwork that exhibits the essence of Japan like how Katsura does.

19. Daitoku-Ji Temple

Address53 MurasakinoDaitokujicho, Kita Ward, Kyoto, Kyoto Prefecture
603-8231 Japan Phone +81 75-491-0019

The Daitoku-Ji Temple, nicknamed as the Zen Temple of Great Virtue, is one of the main temples of the Rinzai sect and was established in the year 1324, with the present structures date back from the 16th and 17th centuries. Of the 22 buildings on-site, seven of them are open to the public, which includes the Kara-mon, a Chinese-style gate with wonderful carvings, and the two-story main gate, Sammon, established in 1589 and famous for its numerous fine statues and ceiling paintings. The Main Hall, the Butsuden, was constructed in the year 1664 and has a statue of Shakyamuni with his disciples Kayo and Anna and a figure of Daito-kokushi, first Abbot of the temple. Beyond the Main Hall is the Lecture Hall, or Hatto, derived from Chinese models, and the Hojo, or Abbot's Lodging, with its wooden tablet, paintings, and connecting garden. Other high spots include the old Abbot's Lodging or Shinju-an with its tombs and statues date back from the 14th century, and a beautiful Zen garden.

The main building of Daitokuji is lined up on the eastern side of the temple grounds in consistent with the traditional layout of a Zen monastery. They're not normally open to the public but visitors might look into the interior of the Butsuden.

The main buildings are walled by almost two dozen sub-temples, a lot of which were added to the compound by medieval lords from throughout Japan. Four of these sub-temples are often open to the public, while some of the others have short-term special openings.

20.   The Byōdō-in Temple

AddressRenge-116 Uji, Kyoto Prefecture611-0021,Japan
Phone+81 774-21-2861

The Byōdō-in Temple dates back to AD 988, boasts a lot of unique shrines, buildings, and artworks that worth your visit. Highlights here include the Phoenix Hall or also known as Hoo-do, which has its bronze phoenixes on its two gables and amusing interior decoration; 11th-century paintings, which includes a magnificent gold-plated figure of Amida; and a ceiling and altar decorated with mother-of-pearl and bronze. Connected to it is the Kannon-do, a hall straight above the river and known as the Fishing Hall or Tsuridono. Make sure to check out the temple gardens with their many nice ponds, as well as the Byōdō-in Museum with its treasures relating to the temple site, which includes the carved phoenixes, 52 wooden Buddha statues, as well as the original temple bell. Also a place you should visit is the Zen Tenryu-Ji Temple, from which you can enter the magnificent Arashiyama Bamboo Grove.

The buildings of Byōdō-in were recurrently lost to fires and other natural disasters over the centuries, but the Phoenix Hall was never wrecked, which makes it one of the few original wooden constructions to survive from the Heian Period. People who visit Byōdō-in can access the Phoenix Hall on short guided tours that start every 20 minutes and cost about ¥ 300. You will find an Amida Buddha statue here.

21.   Kurama and Kifune

Kurama and Kifune is a couple of peaceful rural villages and laid-back and picturesque, only 30-minute train ride to the northern part of Kyoto on Eizan Line. They offer the best half-day trip out of Kyoto.

Address Japan, Kyoto Prefecture, Kyoto, Sakyo Ward □□□□191

Located in the mountains to the north of the Kyoto, going to Kurama and Kifune will make you feel like you are not on the modern Japan. Bounded by wooded mountains, these two picturesque villages will relax your soul after spending too long among the bright neon and modern of the city below. The best attraction is Kurama-dera, a peak temple with spectacular views. Have a side trip by walking to the mountain to the Kifune village.

Kifune-jinja in Sakyo-Ku, Kyoto is the home for about 500 other Kifune shrines situated throughout the country. Constructed approximately 1,600 years ago, the shrine is famous for its long reputation and history. Legend has it that the goddess Tamayori-hime showed up on a yellow boat in Osaka Bay and said, *"Build a sanctuary at the place where this boat stops and defy the spirit of the locality, and the country will prosper."* The boat drifted up the rivers of the Yodo-gawa to the Kamo-gawa, getting a stop at the head of the river.

22.   Sanzenin Temple

Sanzenin Temple is the rural town of Ohara's main highlight, which is situated approximately an hour to the northern part of central Kyoto. The way from Ohara bus stop to Sanzenin is lined with restaurants and shops loved by people visiting the temple, and there are numerous smaller temples in the area. Sanzenin Temple itself has big temple grounds and various buildings, walking paths, and gardens.

Sanzenin is a temple of the Tendai sect of Japanese Buddhism and was established by no other than the respected monk Saicho who presented Tendai Buddhism to the country of Japan in 804. Sanzenin is a monzeki temple, one of only a few temples whose head priests who were members of the imperial family.

Address540 Ohararaikoincho,Sakyo Ward, Kyoto, Kyoto Prefecture601-1242 Japan **Phone** +81 75-744-2531 Once you got to the temple through the front gate, people visiting Sanzenin pass through a sequence of attached temple buildings. The first major building is the Kyakuden, which exhibits works of Japanese paintings and calligraphy on sliding doors. The building opens up onto the Shuhekien Garden, a traditional Japanese garden that has a hill and a little pond.

Linked to the Kyakuden by a corridor, the Shinden shows statues of three Buddhist deities, the figure in the middle is Amida Buddha being skirted by the attendants Fudo Myoo and Kannon. From the Shinden, people can enjoy the most prominent view of Sanzenin Temple: the Ojo Gokuraku-in Hall seen through cedar and maple trees throughout a moss garden.

23. Togetsukyo Bridge

The bridge's name, Togetsu which means "Moon crossing" comes from folklore that when Emperor Kameyama went to ride a boat to cruise the river under a full moon during the Kamakura period, he said the moon resembled like crossing the bridge. The current bridge, reconstructed in the year 1934, appears wooden but has beams and columns all made of strengthened concrete. Only ramparts use cypress. There are many souvenir shops located at the foot of the bridge, while rickshaws commute there, which gives a traditional Japanese feel.

Address Ukyo Ward, Kyoto, Kyoto Prefecture, Japan **Phone** +81 75-871-1339 The Togetsukyo Bridge has been a landmark in Arashiyama District of Western Kyoto for more than 400 years. The wooden bridge spans the Katsura River ahead of Arashiyama Mountain, which offers breathtaking views. The spring cherry blossoms and fall colors attract big crowds, as it offers spectacular scenery.

The bridge was commonly used as setting for ancient Japan-themed movies. It's also a famous place for feeding carp or koi swimming in the river or watching cormorant fishing during the late summer. It's also the place of an important initiation for local children. Young children, both boys, and girls first obtain a blessing from a local temple and then make their way throughout the bridge under orders to do so without looking back. If they ignore the instruction, it's said to carry bad luck consequently, so the risks are high for the believers!

24.   Yasaka Shrine

Yasaka Shrine or also popularly known as Gion Shrine is another famous shrine in Kyoto. Established more than 1350 years ago, the shrine is situated between the popular Higashiyama District and of course, Gion District, and is normally visited by tourists who found themselves between these districts.

The main hall of the shrine combines the inner sanctuary or honden and offering hall or haiden into one building. Ahead of it is where you will find a dance stage with hundreds of lanterns that get set alight in the evenings. Every lantern has the name of a local business who donated them.

Address625 GionmachiKitagawa, HigashiyamaWard, Kyoto, Kyoto Prefecture605-0073 Japan **Phone**+81 75-561-6155   Yasaka Shrine is famous for its summer festival, the Gion Matsuri, which is renowned every month of July. Debatably the most well-known festival in the entire country, the Gion Matsuri was established more than a thousand years and involves a procession with huge floats and hundreds of participants. The shrine also gets busy throughout the cherry blossom season which is around the early month of April, as the neighboring Maruyama Park is one of the most renowned cherry blossom spots in Kyoto.

25.   Kiyomizu-Dera

Kiyomizu-Dera is considered to be the most popular temple in the country. It was established in 780 on the location of the Otowa Waterfall in the forested hills eastern side of Kyoto and gets its name from the pure waters of the falls. The temple was formerly related to the Hosso sect, one of the oldest schools of Japanese Buddhism, but shaped its own Kita Hosso sect in the year 1965. In 1994, the temple was added as one of UNESCO World Heritage Sites.

Address 294 Kiyomizu 1-chome, Higashiyama Ward, Kyoto, Kyoto Prefecture 605-0862, Japan **Phone** +81 75-551-1234 The veranda of the temple juts out of the mountain side reinforced by 13-meter-high wooden pillars. The main hall with its unique hip-shaped roof of cypress wood rests to the hindmost of the veranda and inside you will find a precious statue of Kannon Bodhisattva, the goddess of mercy. From the veranda, you can enjoy beautiful views that face west over the city of Kyoto. It's also an amazing place to watch the sunset, which may also the reason why the romantic relations rendered to the temple.

Within the vicinity is where you can also find the Jishu-jinja Shrine, and some people believe that when they pray there, there will be a better chance for them to find their love match. People eager to find their love match can be seen walking between two bulbous stones while their eyes are closed.

Shopping Around

Kyoto is well-known for temples, but also as a paradise for people who love shopping. Here is a list of some of the best shops in Kyoto and some useful tips.

Kyoto is a nice place to buy both modern and traditional Japanese products. Actually, it is possibly easier to shop here than other cities in Japan like Tokyo, since Kyoto is dense and most of the shopping places are situated just right downtown, all within just a quick walk from the main subway stations.

Key Areas

The main shopping districts in Kyoto are found around the area where the streets of Kawaramachi-dori and Shijo-dori meet. Going here you will find giant department stores. The place between Karasuma-dori and Kawaramachi-dori has smaller, independent individual shops and boutiques that sell both traditional products and the newest fashion styles. Stylish shops, high-class boutiques, and chic restaurants can also be found throughout the sophisticated Kitayama Street, which expanses eastward from Kitayama Bridge further to the northern part of Kyoto.

Kyoto has numerous shops that offer handmade Japanese paper, and Morita Washi, Higashinotoin-dori-Bukkoji again, close to the Shijo-dori, is the most popular, selling purified paper of the utmost quality. Japanese movies and comic fans should go to Teramachi-dori, one of largest shopping arcades in Kyoto, which runs between Shijo-dori and Oike, where there are some stores specializing in anime and manga.

Markets

Kyoto is well-known for the shops that sell arts and crafts, and the best one a tourist can check out is certainly the multi-stored Kyoto Handicraft Center, which is selling an extensive variety of souvenirs particularly handicraft products, from lacquer ware, jewelry, porcelain, fabrics and woodblock prints to swords, kimonos, and shirts. Another exceptional craft shop is found in the Kyoto Craft Center, which has displays of ceramics, textiles, and a lot of other types of craft items made by local artists and craftsmen.

Shopping Centers

There are some big department stores between Kawaramachi-dori and Shijo-dori, where you'll find big high-street brands and other fashion chain stores.

Souvenirs

The hollow, implausible station is home to a sequence of brilliant souvenir shops which sell not only your average key rings and fridge magnets. The Cube mall, in the basement of the station, is the perfect spot to buy gifts for your family and friends back home, particularly if you are about to hop on a bullet train or *shinkansen* to your following destination.

Tax Information

A tax consumption of 5% is added to the worth of all the products. Credit cards are gradually becoming more broadly accepted, but most transactions are still paid in cash.

Nightlife

What's better than a fine summer evening spent walking on the beautiful streets of Kyoto? From the district of Gion where you can find geisha walking around to the restaurants and bars line up is absolutely romantic and charming at night. Start with a walk throughout the banks of Kamo River – this is particularly a perfect place for young lovers looking for a romantic night stroll. During the summer season, you will find restaurants stretching from north and south of Shijo Dori throughout the river erect outdoor platforms made of wood on stilts throughout the water.

Though the nightlife in Kyoto is calmer than Osaka's, the areas throughout the old geisha quarters downtown flourish with bars and nightclubs. The Kiyamachi region throughout the little canal close to Pontocho in central Kyoto is filled with restaurants, bars, and some nightclubs and is as near a combined nightlife area as you will get in Kyoto. It is filled little watering holes with red lanterns or small neon signs ahead. It is also enjoyable to stroll around the Gion in the eastern part of Kyoto and Pontocho in central Kyoto to try to get a sight of a geisha or maiko walking down the alleyway on their way to or from an appointment.

There are a lot of yearly events and dances, which include the really popular geisha dances, took place in June, the only time of year you could see traditional dances done by all five of traditional geisha districts in Kyoto.

The Major Nightlife Districts

Gion - A little neighborhood of plain wooden buildings in Higashiyama-Ku on the east side of the Kamo River, Gion does not look anything like what you have probably come to expect about a city Japanese nightlife area; actually, there is a little neon just around the corner. There is something almost solemn and austere about the most famous geisha district of Kyoto, as though its purpose were markedly more important and consecrated than mere entertainment. Gion is a sanctuary to the past of Kyoto, and the period when geisha totaled in the thousands.

Counter to popular misconceptions of the West, geisha aren't prostitutes. Instead, they are trained professionals in conversation, the traditional arts, and coquettishness, and their main role is to make men feel like they are kings when they are in the calming territory of the geisha house. There are now just about 200 geisha in Gion; after all, in the high-tech world of today, only a few women are eager to experience the years of hard training to learn tea ceremony, to play a three-stringed instrument called *shamisen*, or to carry out early court dances.

Gion is approximately a 5-minute walk from the intersection of Shijo-Kawaramachi; to be able to get here, walk to the east on Shijo Dori and then go right on Hanamikoji Dori. The narrow streets are a nice place for strolling; a nice time to take a stroll the neighborhood is around twilight when geisha are seen walking to their appointments. Geisha are dressed in a bright kimono, while chalky white face and hair decorated with ornaments and hairpins.

Pontocho - Pontocho is a narrow alley that matches the western bank or Kamo River, stretching from Shijo Dori north to Sanjo Dori. Once riddled with geisha houses and other members-only establishments, it's now lined with clubs, bars, restaurants, and hostess bars that fill all nook and crannies. Pontocho makes for a captivating walk as you watch groups of Japanese enjoying the night away.

Another nice place to spend is **Kiyamachi** (https://en.yelp.com.ph/biz/kiyamachi-sakuragawa- 京都市,) which is another little street that parallels Pontocho just to the west and runs beside a little canal.

The Bar Scene

Kushi Kura (https://en.yelp.com.ph/biz/ 串くら - 本店 - 京都市) and **Ichiba Kouji** (https://en.yelp.com.ph/biz/ 市場小路 - 京都市) are nice spots to get a drink or two.

Local Life

The city of Kyoto is where the old and new collide wherever you look. Kyoto today is a modern Japanese city with an unbelievable amount of living traditions and rich history.

Though Kyoto is known for its traditional neighborhood, not all of Kyoto is as pretty, delightful neighborhood that will give you an old feel. While there are some well-preserved old districts throughout the city and the surrounding regions, most of the city looks just like any other modern city in Japan, with neon, concrete, pachinko parlors, and convenience stores. But there are the incredible thing you can find almost anywhere you look at, and this is one of the best things about living here.

If you want to go to a bit distance, you can easily hop the buses, which are abundant and crisscross through a section of the city or simply hop on the subway, which is nowhere near as broad as Tokyo's, but useful nevertheless. Kyoto is also a nice city for the cycling, as it is just compact and relaxed enough to make for easy and tranquil biking from a place to another.

But walking is a lot more fun to do. During the winter season, locals like to walk long distances and then warm up in restaurants, cafes, or comfortable Japanese-style gastropubs or izakaya.

Japan is an extremely modern country, and it's one of the countries in the world with fast internet, but Kyoto lags behind the rest of Japan. Most cafes in the city do not offer access to Wi-Fi, so if you think going to Starbucks would be a nice choice for you, think again.

There are a lot of Starbucks in the central part of Kyoto, with shops dotted all over the city center. But if you happen to find a coffee shop that offers free access to the internet, they can be a little strict about plugging your device to their power outlet.

Old Japanese homes are infamous for the absence of insulation. So, the locals normally keep themselves warm during the winter season by taking a bath in the evening. Japanese people love baths, so if you stay in a local's house, no matter how old it is, you can expect for it to have a nice little bath, that has temperature controls, and different buttons to give you the temperature perfect for you. You can set the water temperature for as hot as you want, which make it the ideal way to warm up in chilly winter of Kyoto.

Locals love their meal with sake or beer and you often they cook their own meals at home as it is relatively cheaper. Another thing the city boasts is their reputation for having the best matcha desserts and tofu.

Kyoto isn't a small city, but only 30 to 60 minutes away from Osaka and pretty larger, which has both unbelievable food and unique, interesting nightlife. Kyoto is also close to the city of Nara, Kobe, Mount Koya, and a lot more. Not to mention it is only less than three from Tokyo when you ride the bullet train.

Another thing that is loved by the locals about Kyoto is the great high level of safety and the pure kindness of the people even strangers.

Kyoto isn't always the top-of-the-mind place to go when travelers are planning a trip to Japan. It's usually because people don't understand how stunning that city is, or perhaps people don't prefer the less multicultural part of the country. The antique capital of Japan is one of the most interesting places you can go in your lifetime, a lot of things to discover, a lot of things to learn, and a lot of things to experience.

Local Life

The city of Kyoto is where the old and new collide wherever you look. Kyoto today is a modern Japanese city with an unbelievable amount of living traditions and rich history.

Though Kyoto is known for its traditional neighborhood, not all of Kyoto is as pretty, delightful neighborhood that will give you an old feel. While there are some well-preserved old districts throughout the city and the surrounding regions, most of the city looks just like any other modern city in Japan, with neon, concrete, pachinko parlors, and convenience stores. But there are the incredible thing you can find almost anywhere you look at, and this is one of the best things about living here.

If you want to go to a bit distance, you can easily hop the buses, which are abundant and crisscross through a section of the city or simply hop on the subway, which is nowhere near as broad as Tokyo's, but useful nevertheless. Kyoto is also a nice city for the cycling, as it is just compact and relaxed enough to make for easy and tranquil biking from a place to another.

But walking is a lot more fun to do. During the winter season, locals like to walk long distances and then warm up in restaurants, cafes, or comfortable Japanese-style gastropubs or izakaya.

Japan is an extremely modern country, and it's one of the countries in the world with fast internet, but Kyoto lags behind the rest of Japan. Most cafes in the city do not offer access to Wi-Fi, so if you think going to Starbucks would be a nice choice for you, think again.

There are a lot of Starbucks in the central part of Kyoto, with shops dotted all over the city center. But if you happen to find a coffee shop that offers free access to the internet, they can be a little strict about plugging your device to their power outlet.

Old Japanese homes are infamous for the absence of insulation. So, the locals normally keep themselves warm during the winter season by taking a bath in the evening. Japanese people love baths, so if you stay in a local's house, no matter how old it is, you can expect for it to have a nice little bath, that has temperature controls, and different buttons to give you the temperature perfect for you. You can set the water temperature for as hot as you want, which make it the ideal way to warm up in chilly winter of Kyoto.

Locals love their meal with sake or beer and you often they cook their own meals at home as it is relatively cheaper. Another thing the city boasts is their reputation for having the best matcha desserts and tofu.

Kyoto isn't a small city, but only 30 to 60 minutes away from Osaka and pretty larger, which has both unbelievable food and unique, interesting nightlife. Kyoto is also close to the city of Nara, Kobe, Mount Koya, and a lot more. Not to mention it is only less than three from Tokyo when you ride the bullet train.

Another thing that is loved by the locals about Kyoto is the great high level of safety and the pure kindness of the people even strangers.

Kyoto isn't always the top-of-the-mind place to go when travelers are planning a trip to Japan. It's usually because people don't understand how stunning that city is, or perhaps people don't prefer the less multicultural part of the country. The antique capital of Japan is one of the most interesting places you can go in your lifetime, a lot of things to discover, a lot of things to learn, and a lot of things to experience.

Made in the USA
Las Vegas, NV
10 February 2024

85625654R00077